PORTF
# THE WORLD OF THE

KANAKALATHA MUKUND holds a doctorate in economics and was on the faculty of the University of Bombay, Bhopal University and the Centre for Economic and Social Studies, Hyderabad. An economist with a keen interest in history and a passion for textiles, she is the author of *The Trading World of the Tamil Merchant*, *The View from Below* and *Traditional Industry in the New Market Economy*. She lives in Coonoor in the Nilgiris.

GURCHARAN DAS is a world-renowned author, commentator and public intellectual. His bestselling books include *India Unbound*, *The Difficulty of Being Good* and *India Grows at Night*. His other literary works consist of a novel, *A Fine Family*, a book of essays, *The Elephant Paradigm*, and an anthology, *Three Plays*. A graduate of Harvard University, Das was CEO of Procter & Gamble, India, before he took early retirement to become a full-time writer. He lives in Delhi.

THE STORY OF INDIAN BUSINESS
Series Editor: Gurcharan Das

THE STORY OF INDIAN BUSINESS
Series Editor: Gurcharan Das

# THE STORY OF INDIAN BUSINESS

# THE WORLD OF THE
# TAMIL MERCHANT

*Pioneers of International Trade*

## KANAKALATHA MUKUND

*Introduction by*
## Gurcharan Das

PORTFOLIO
PENGUIN

An imprint of Penguin Random House

PORTFOLIO

USA | Canada | UK | Ireland | Australia
New Zealand | India | South Africa | China

Portfolio is part of the Penguin Random House group of companies
whose addresses can be found at global.penguinrandomhouse.com

Published by Penguin Random House India Pvt. Ltd
7th Floor, Infinity Tower C, DLF Cyber City,
Gurgaon 122 002, Haryana, India

Penguin
Random House
India

First published as *The Merchants of Tamilakam* in Allen Lane by Penguin
Books India 2012
Published under the present title in Portfolio 2015

ISBN 9780143424734

Typeset in Aldine401 BT by SŪRYA, New Delhi
Printed at Repro Knowledgecast Limited, India

www.penguin.co.in

MIX
Paper from
responsible sources
FSC® C047271

# CONTENTS

# CONTENTS

vi

# List of Illustrations

# List of Maps

# INTRODUCTION

> In [Puhar] lived many merchants who brought in
> wonderful and expensive goods from other countries
> across the seas on large ships and overland on carts
> and carried on their trade here.
>
> —*Silappadikaram*, I.ii.5–7

## The story of Indian business

The south has always had this advantage over the north.
South India has a coastline, which means access to high
seas and world trade via rich ports. Kanakalatha
Mukund's masterly study of commerce in the Tamil
country proves the value of a coast and the veracity of
the old saying that nations that engage in trade will be
more prosperous. Her ambitious study covers a period
of more than a thousand years, from the Sangam age

(first to third century CE), with its rich storehouse of epics like *Silappadikaram* and *Manimekalai*, to the end of the Chola Empire in the thirteenth century. Like other books in Penguin's multi-volume story of Indian business, it is based on a close examination of texts and inscriptions, seeking to mine great ideas in business and economics that have shaped commerce on the Indian subcontinent.

In this series leading contemporary scholars interpret texts and ideas in a lively, sharp and authoritative manner for the intelligent reader with no prior background in the field. Each slender volume recounts the romance and adventure of business enterprise in the bazaar or on the high seas. Each author offers an enduring perspective on business and economic enterprise in the past, avoiding the pitfall of simplistically cataloguing a set of lessons for today. The value of the exercise, if we are successful, will be to promote in the reader a longer-term sensibility, which can help to understand the material bases for our present human condition and to think sensibly about the future. Taken together, the series as a whole celebrates the ideal captured in the Sanskrit word *artha*, 'material well-being', which was one of the aims of the classical Indian life.

The books in this series range over a vast territory, beginning more than 2000 years ago with the renowned

Tom Trautman's book on the ancient art of wealth, *Arthashastra*, and ending with the *Bombay Plan*, drawn by eminent industrialists in 1944–45 who wrestled with the proper roles of the public and private sectors—all their debates are brought alive by Medha Kudaisiya. In between there is a veritable feast. In addition to the *Arthashastra* and this volume, three sparkling books cover the ancient and early medieval periods—Gregory Schopen presents the *Business Model of Early Buddhist Monasticism* based on the *Mulasarvastivada-vinaya*; Himanshu Prabha Ray transfers us to the maritime trading world of the western Indian Ocean, along the Kanara and Gujarat coasts, using the Sanskrit *Lekhapaddhati* written in Gujarati; and Arshia Sattar recounts the brilliant adventures of *The Mouse Merchant* and other tales based on *Kathasaritsagara* and other sources.

Scott Levi takes off from the early modern period with the saga of Multani traders in caravans through central Asia over 500 years, rooted in the work of Zia al-Din Barani's *Tarikh-i Firuz Shahi* and Jean-Baptiste Tavernier. The celebrated Sanjay Subrahmanyam and Muzaffar Alam transport us into the world of sultans, shopkeepers and portfolio capitalists in Mughal India. Ishan Chakrabarti traces the ethically individualistic world of Banarsidas, a Jain merchant in Mughal times, via his diary, *Ardhakathanak*. Tirthankar Roy's elegant volume on the East India Company is our passage into the modern world, where the distinguished Lakshmi Subramanian recounts the ups and downs in the adventurous lives of three great merchants of Bombay—Tarwady Arjunjee Nathjee, Jamsetjee Jeejeebhoy and Premchand Raychand.

Anuradha Kumar adds to this a narrative on the building of railways in nineteenth-century India through the eyes of those who built them. Chhaya Goswami dives deep into the Indian Ocean to recount the tale of Kachchhi enterprise in the triangle between Zanzibar, Muscat and Mandvi. Tom Timberg revisits the bold, risk-taking world of the Marwaris and Raman Mahadevan describes the Nattukottai Chettiars' search for fortune. Vikramjit Banerjee rounds up the series with competing visions of prosperity among men who fought for India's freedom in the early twentieth century through the works of Gandhi, Vivekenanda, Nehru, Ambedkar, and others. The privilege of reading these rich and diverse volumes has left me—one reader—with a sense of wonder at the vivid, dynamic and illustrious role played by trade and economic enterprise in advancing Indian civilization.

# The 'sink of the world's metal'

One of the recurring themes in this series is the constant flow of gold and silver from the West to India. Romans complained 2000 years ago that their trade with India was draining their empire of bullion. The Portuguese protested in the sixteenth century that their hard-won silver from South America was being lost to India. The British Parliament echoed this refrain in the seventeenth century and asked why the East India Company could not interest Indians to buy more British goods. The fact is that consumers in the West have long hankered after Indian spices and luxuries but Indians were not particularly interested in western things; since books had to be balanced, they were balanced with gold and silver, and this meant a drain of precious metal from the West. It was only in the early nineteenth century that the bullion flow changed direction. This is one of the themes I should like to explore in this introduction.

Soon after reading Kanakalatha Mukund's book, I stumbled onto a story in my newspaper in mid 2011 about the discovery of a fabulous treasure. With one vault still to be opened, the treasure found in the Sree Padmanabha temple at Thiruvananthapuram in Kerala had been initially valued at over Rs 1,00,000 crore ($22 billion), surpassing the riches of the famed Tirupati temple or any other religious spot for that matter. Life may be different everywhere but the human heart is the same, and it is drawn to riches. The story spread like fire around the world, inviting a universal reaction of awe, mystery and bafflement. What was one to make of the treasure? This book holds some answers.

Among the treasures found was a vast store of gold coins of the Roman Empire called Aureus as well as Greek Drachmas; Venetian gold ducats of the fourteenth and fifteenth centuries when Venice was a great maritime power; Portuguese currency from the days of its glory in the sixteenth century; seventeenth-century coins of the Dutch East India and eighteenth-century coins of the British East India Company; Napoleon's gold coins from the early nineteenth century; and much more. It was a veritable feast of India's economic history. How did the world's bullion end up in the vaults of a temple in south India?

India has always been a maritime, trading nation. With a 5000-mile coastline, it has had a class of adventurous, seafaring merchants who traded across the seas. The constant flow of precious metal into India was a part of this trading pattern, as already pointed out. Roman senators grumbled that their women used too many Indian spices and luxuries which drained the Roman Empire of precious metal. Pliny the Elder, in 77 CE, called India 'the sink of the world's precious metal' in his encyclopaedic work on classical Rome, *Naturalis Historia*, in which he describes his voyage from Alexandria across the Indian Ocean to the famed port of Muziris, near Cochin in south India.

Rome consumed more than she produced and a large part of the drain of gold and silver which Pliny speaks of went to south India, especially to the east and west coasts of the Deccan. As a result, rich hoards of Roman coins have been found buried in many coastal Indian sites. Following Nero's death, the Roman Emperor Vespasian passed a series of laws to curb the luxurious lifestyle of the upper classes, and luxury imports from India were banned. After that the Roman trade with India was confined mostly to lower-value commodities such as pepper and textiles. But the trade imbalance continued and Roman coins moved rapidly in Indian bazaars. Unprecedented prosperity was generated by the Roman trade in India, raising the demand for currency. Since Roman coins were trusted, they supplemented the local supply. Kanishka, who ruled Punjab and the north-west, melted Roman coins and modelled his on them. To manage the drain of gold, Septimius Severus (193–211 CE) reduced the gold content in Roman coins, thus debasing the currency, and this explains why so few Roman coins have been found in India after Septimius. The drain, however, shifted to the east as the Byzantine Empire began to protest that their reserves of precious metals were 'leaked away to India'.

When the Europeans rediscovered India in 1498, they prudently brought silver and gold, acquired from the mines of their new colonies in America. On returning home from his voyage to India, Vasco da Gama told King Manuel of Portugal that he had seen 'large cities, large buildings and rivers, and great populations'. But he added that Indians were not interested in European trinkets and clothes. François Bernier, the French physician to the Mughal emperor Aurangzeb in the seventeenth century, confirmed the drain in his travel diary: 'It should not escape notice that gold and silver, after circulating in every other quarter of the globe, come at length to be absorbed in Hindostan'. Thus, Indian demand for precious metals continued in exchange particularly for luxury textiles—calico, muslin, chintz, bandana—and these legendary names gradually entered into European languages. Bernier's compatriot Baron de Montesquieu pretty much summed up the situation in 1748: 'Every nation, that ever traded with the Indies, has constantly carried bullion, and brought merchandises in return . . . They want, therefore, nothing but our bullion.'

This pattern continued till the nineteenth century

when the flow reversed suddenly. The conquest of India by East India Company may have been a factor but the main reason for the reversal was the Industrial Revolution in Britain. It brought machine-made textiles which rendered Indian handlooms obsolete. Indians had finally found something they wanted from the West—cheap, durable cottons from the mills of Lancashire. Handlooms all over the world gave way to machine-made cloth, and since India was the world's largest producer of handlooms its weavers suffered the most. This reverse flow of drain to Britain persisted until textile mills came up in India and began to satisfy local demand. By 1936 they fulfilled 62 per cent of the demand.

To return to Padmanabha's treasure: the vast hoard of foreign gold coins thus came to India through trade routes, especially to the rich port cities of south India. In chapter four, Kanakalatha Mukund explains how it might have ended up in a temple. With the recovery of Hinduism in the sixth century CE, the temple emerged as a vibrant centre of religious, economic and social life. For centuries Buddhism and Jainism had become the dominant religions, but the energy behind the bhakti movement revived Hinduism. Mukund explains how kings, merchants and landlords supported temples with generous donations of gold, silver and precious stones, not only to gain *punyam*, religious merit, but also legitimacy in the eyes of the people. The medieval village assembly, the 'sabha', met on the temple's premises, with the deity presiding, possessed of legal powers.

I shall return to the temple treasure at the end of the introduction, but let us turn now to a second theme.

## The state, the merchant and society

Economic and business success needs a predictable political environment. Political stability gives private individuals the confidence to invest, and this leads to capital accumulation, which in turn promotes prosperity and economic development. Kanakalatha Mukund's discussion on the long reign of the Tamil monarchs and dynasties confirms this. It is also a nice corrective to the common prejudice about the instability of Indian history—sometimes viewed as an intolerable series of internecine wars among nasty, petty kingdoms. Monarchy does not get good press these days, but Mukund, as well as Tom Trautmann in his volume on the *Arthashastra*, has restored some balance. Since the average reign of monarchs and dynasties was long, this meant peace and stability of political power.

The main forms of government in ancient India were

the kingdom and the *sangha*, republic. The republic had the advantage in the solidarity of its governing class, according to the *Arthashastra*, but the kingdom had economic advantages, and hence it has prevailed in history. This advantage rested primarily on its 'greater ability to amass capital through taxation and economic enterprise'. I argued in my introduction to the *Arthashastra*, the Indian king, far from being an 'Oriental despot' of the Aristotelian variety, did not own all the land in the kingdom but only had a *bhaga*, share, of the land, and it was usually a sixth. Trautmann calls the concept of bhaga entrepreneurial for 'the focus is not on ownership of a resource but of a share of what is produced ... [and] at the heart of the idea of the share [is] a certain sense of mutual interest among co-sharers to promote production, as then all shares will be larger'.

Although the record of inscriptions may suggest otherwise, the underlying history of India has been surprisingly stable and the kingdoms themselves have endured for centuries. From the dissolution of the Gupta Empire around 550 CE till the Turkish Sultanate of Delhi just after 1200 CE, Trautmann calculates that the 'average length of a king's reign was not much less than the average length of a generation (25 years) ... [and] many royal dynasties ruled for hundreds of years. Among the longest are the Eastern Chalukyas, a buffer state in the Deccan, which lasted 400 years. The reign of the Palas of Bengal and the Cholas of the South endured for over 300 years.' Regional powers kept fighting to wrest control of buffer areas, but the kingdoms themselves were stable and their economic policies, which financed them, were successful on the whole.

Two major empires emerged in the Tamil region after the sixth century, the Pallavas in the north who ruled from Kanchipuram and the Pandyas in the south from Madurai. The Cholas, who had stood on the margins of history until the mid ninth century, rose to become the premier power of south India and ruled till the end of the thirteenth century. The centuries of Pallava peace led to the development of the great port of Mamallapuram filled with boats 'carrying treasure which captivated the senses, and elephants and loads of precious stones'. During the Chola peace, the port of Nagapattinam superseded Mamallapuram. Both ports were situated on the coast of Coromandel—which is an Anglicization of Cholamandalam—and were symbols of the economic rise of the Tamil country.

The success of the Tamil state lay in its robust local institutions of governance which predated the Pallavas and the Cholas, who sensibly left these institutions alone. The village had its *ur* and *sabha*; the sub-region the *nadu*; the district its *kottam*; and the town or city had its *nagaram*, which dealt with commercial disputes between merchants, among other things. They were run through a democratic 'assembly' of citizens in an egalitarian manner and went a long way in giving legitimacy to the kings. Nevertheless, the power of the impressive Pallava and Chola states was not enough to provide sufficient security to the merchant who had to travel long distances. *The World of the Tamil Merchant* shows this vividly in the account of the warrior merchant and the private security provided by the powerful guild, the Five Hundred.

The power of the Pallava and the Chola states, while noteworthy in the Indian context, was no match for the Chinese empire, which was the pre-eminent power in the region. The rulers of South-East Asia acknowledged its superior status and sent it tribute regularly. So did the Pallava ruler Narasimhavarman II—he sent an embassy in 720 CE. The Chola rulers followed and sent regular embassies to the Chinese court—Rajaraja I in 1015 CE; Rajendra in 1033 CE; and Kulottunga in 1077 CE.

A comparison with China is useful as it throws light on the Indian state. The truth is that India has never allowed state power to be as concentrated as in China, so that it could reach deeply and change its basic social institutions. The type of despotic governments that emerged in China (and Russia), which were able to divest the whole society of property and personal rights, have never existed in south Asia. Not surprisingly, India's history is by and large one of competing political kingdoms, while China's is one of strong empires.

India has always had a weak state and a strong society, and a recent book, *The Origins of Political Order* by Francis Fukuyama, explains the difference with China nicely. Political authority in India was either too distant or irrelevant to the daily life of Indian society. What has held India together over the centuries is its society. Jawaharlal Nehru, in *The Discovery of India*, defined this society in three words: village, caste and family. It consisted of more than half a million autonomous, self-sufficient villages; over 2000 hierarchical *jati*s, sub-castes; and the joint family. What is significant about this society, Nehru felt, is not only hierarchy, but the idea that the group is more important than the individual. The individual's freedom in India was limited not so much by the state as by kinship ties, caste rules, religious obligations and custom. The tyranny of cousins allowed Indians to resist the tyranny of tyrants. A strong society helped to balance and keep in check the state.

Social actors in China, on the other hand, have always been much weaker than in India. They were much less able to resist a state that was much more powerful. This contrast was just as obvious in the third century BCE, when Qin Shih Huangdi and Ashoka were building their empires, as it is today. Protests against social injustice in India historically were not aimed at the state as in China. These were aimed at the social order, dominated by the Brahmins, and were expressed as dissident religious movements like Buddhism, Jainism and the bhakti sects.

The Indian state evolved from a tribal society in the middle of the first millennium BCE in northern India. From the beginning, the tribal raja's authority was limited by sabhas or *samitis* of his kinsmen. The land did not belong to the king but to clan families, such as the Kurus and Panchalas in the epic *Mahabharata*. The raja did not own land, nor had taxing authority in the modern sense; ownership was vested in the clan. Even when sovereign states emerged in the sixth century BCE, like Magadha, the king's power continued to be limited by dharma or the law, and by Brahmins who interpreted the law. The law did not spring from the king as it did in China, but was above the monarch, who was expected to protect dharma, as the *Dharmashastras* make clear. The raja who violates dharma is called a 'mad dog' in the *Mahabharata*, and the epic encourages a revolt against him.

China's state also emerged from tribal society around

the same time in the first millennium BCE. The trajectories diverged, however. India never experienced centuries-long continuous violence comparable to China's Spring and Autumn wars or the Warring States periods. The reason for this is unclear. Fukuyama speculates that it might be that the density of population in the Indus and Gangetic river valleys was much lower than in China. If people felt coerced, they simply migrated rather than submit to the whim of a tyrannical king. In China, on the other hand, a strong state developed over the centuries. It was able to carry out tasks that India could not, from building a Great Wall for keeping out nomadic invaders to mounting huge hydroelectric projects in the twenty-first century like the Three Gorges Dam.

Not surprisingly, India became a chaotic democracy after Independence. In the 1960s Gunnar Myrdal called it a 'soft state'. Today, India seems to be rising from below, marching towards a modern, democratic and market-based future without too much help from the state. It is quite unlike China, whose success has been scripted from above by a technocratic state under the communist party that has built incredible infrastructure.

A successful nation, however, needs both a strong state and a strong society. A strong state is obviously not an oppressive state but an effective one which implements its laws fairly. A weak state has a weak rule of law and tolerates corruption, and this creates uncertainty in people's minds. People obey the law in a free society because they think that it is fair and applies to everyone equally. But if policemen, ministers and judges can be bought, then people lose confidence in the rule of law. A 'weak state' with widespread corruption poses this danger in contemporary India.

## Temples and treasures

The most remarkable feature of *The World of the Tamil Merchant* is its account of the central role of the temple in the economic, social and political life of south India. In Mukund's words, the temple 'was a major player in the economy in its own right. More importantly, it became a depository institution which attracted donations of gold, money, land and livestock as well as deposits of money. Both were circulated in the local economy on well-specified terms of interest to be paid in kind to maintain temple services, and in the process the temple became the medium for redistributing the surplus which came under its control. By participating in donations and temple management, merchants and larger associations of nagaram and guild earned social acceptance and recognition.'

Mukund could have added 'the king' to merchants and nagarams, who sought legitimacy in the people's eyes when they honoured the temple. And this legitimacy was crucial to the exercise of economic, social and political power. One such king was the frugal Varma ruler of the old Travancore state who left his wealth to the Padmanabha temple for safe-keeping. Padmanabha is another name for the god Vishnu, whose exquisite reclining statue made from 32 kilos of pure gold was recovered among the temple treasures. Although the temple has existed for a thousand years, it became rich and famous after the local ruler Marthanda Varma defeated a Dutch army in the battle of Kulachal in 1771. Thereafter, he and his successors dedicated their kingdom to Padmanabha, donating lavishly to the temple. So did all his successors. Even today, his descendant supervises the temple trust as a servant of Padmanabha, a *dasa*.

In January 2011, the Kerala High Court rejected the contention that Sree Padmanabha was a family temple of the royal family and ordered the government to establish a state trust to manage the temple. The Supreme Court, however, stayed the high court's judgement, and passed an interim order asking a special investigating team to document what was in the temple's vaults. This is how the treasure was discovered in July 2011.

It is appropriate, however, that the treasure was discovered on the twentieth anniversary of India's economic reforms, which finally forced open its economy after forty years. Soon after Independence, India's leaders forgot about their nation's grand trading heritage and closed its economy in the mistaken belief that trade and foreign capital were responsible for the people's impoverishment under the British Raj. They were pessimistic about India's ability to compete in the world economy. Touting the mantra of 'self-reliance', they adopted an inward-looking, import-substituting path rather than an outward-looking, export-promoting route. Thus, they lost a huge opportunity to ride on an unprecedented trading boom in the global economy after World War II, which brought unparalleled prosperity to those nations that remained open. India's share of world trade declined from 2.2 per cent in 1947 to 0.5 per cent in 1990. It is only after the reforms in 1991 that India began to regain its historic pre-eminence as a trading nation and to rise again economically.

The historic drain of precious metal into India and Padmanabha's treasure raise questions that have engaged economists for decades. Given the one-way flow of gold and silver into India over the centuries, a staggering amount has accumulated and lies buried or in vaults across the country. The amount estimated to be above the ground is between 25,000 to 30,000 tonnes, more than twice that of any other country. Moreover, India continues to be the destination for a quarter to a third of the world's annual gold flow, according to the World Gold Council. The reason for India's fascination for gold, Trautmann speculates, goes back to the old institution of *stridhana*, woman's wealth. It is what a woman takes with her into marriage, in lieu of the father's inheritance to sons, and it is in the form of gold jewellery. This practice continues since ancient times although the inheritance law for daughters has changed after Independence.

How can one transform this asset so that it remains a safe social security—often of a poor woman—but is also available to the national economy for productive investment? To a modest extent gold loans or gold bonds are step in this direction. However, the opportunity is massive. It is a challenge for entrepreneurs and regulators to devise safe, liquid instruments, like annuities, which consumers could purchase with gold and silver, and which could be linked to the value of the metal as a guarantee against inflation and returnable on demand.

As to what should be done with Padmanabha's treasure: clearly, it should not be reburied. The donors should not object to investing it wisely in sovereign instruments, using only the income from the capital. One possibility is to run schools, colleges and hospitals for the poor. Another is to set up a museum beside the magnificent temple. One could probably do both given the size of the corpus. A world-class museum dedicated to India's maritime trading tradition, designed by a great, renowned architect will draw tourists from around the world and do wonders for the city's economy. It would also provide devotees darshana of god's ornaments, and be a symbol of their bhakti. The town of Bilbao in northern Spain was unknown until the great Frank Gehry built a stunning museum there, and now the world flocks to pay homage to it. But this idea will only succeed if it is not managed by bureaucrats of the Archaeological Survey of India, under whose charge our present museum treasures collect dust instead of inspiring wonder. A privately managed museum might also inspire philanthropic sentiments in the new breed of Indian billionaires.

GURCHARAN DAS

# AUTHOR'S NOTE

THIS BOOK IS about Tamilakam, the land of the Tamil people. I have retained this in preference to Tamil Nadu throughout the book. Though both words mean the same, Tamil Nadu is now a political entity in a modern nation state, whereas Tamilakam refers to the linguistic and cultural identity of a people, dating back to ancient times.

This work is based on published Tamil literary works and inscriptions. All the material in Tamil cited in the book has been translated by me. Tamil words are transliterated as they are pronounced, rather than the more orthographically correct mode. Thus, I have used hard and soft consonants—'k' and 'g', 't' and 'd', 'p' and 'b'—though there is only one letter for both sounds in Tamil, and also 'j', 'h' and 's' which do not exist in the Tamil alphabet. For ease of reading, since Tamil does not have aspirated consonants, I have used Chola and Chera, rather than the more correct forms of Cola and Cera. I have not used diacritical marks in the interests of better readability.

I would like to thank Gurcharan Das and Penguin India for asking me to undertake this work, which has given me a great opportunity to revisit my roots. I would like to express my gratitude to various friends who have helped me in this effort. Dr R. Champakalakshmi was helpful with suggestions, which have been of great value. I would like to add a special word of thanks to Dr P. Shanmugam for generously sharing with me many rare publications which I would not have been able to access otherwise. My daughter, Janaki Mukund, and Chandra Chari of *The Book Review*, New Delhi, were most forthcoming in their readiness to help with references. I owe a great debt to my son-in-law, Srikumar Natarajan, for all his help with the illustrations.

I would also like to thank Dr Lakshmi Subramanian and Gurcharan Das for their suggestions and comments which have been very useful in revising the work.

# CHRONOLOGY OF TAMIL HISTORY

**268 BCE – 233 BCE** Asoka, Mauryan emperor. Rock-cut edicts in south India refer to the Tamil kingdoms.

**1st–3rd century** CE Satavahana kingdom extending from the Deccan to north India.

**50–300 CE** Commonly referred to as the Sangam age in the history of Tamilakam. Anthologies of poems from the third Sangam. Tamilakam ruled by the 'three kings'—Chola, Chera and Pandya—and many smaller chiefs. Extensive trade with Rome/Mediterranean regions in the west and South-East Asia to the east.

**75 CE** Pliny's *Natural History*; *Periplus of the Erythrean Sea*.

**78 CE** Kanishka became the Kushan emperor, marking the beginning of the Saka era.

**125 CE** Ptolemy's *Guide to Geography*.

**319–455 CE** Gupta empire in the north.

**300–550** CE 'Kalabhra interregnum' in Tamilakam, marked by absence of historical records. Spread of Jainism and Buddhism in the region. Tamil epics *Silappadikaram* and *Manimekalai* and the work on ethics *Tirukkural* written during this period.

**Early 5th century** CE Rise of Hindu kingdoms of South-East Asia: Kambuja and Champa.

**550–900** CE Rise of the Tamil kingdoms. Pallavas in northern Tamilakam with their capital at Kanchipuram and Pandyas in southern Tamilakam, with their capital at Madurai.

    *Major Pallava kings*

    **555–590** CE Simhavishnu

    **590–630** CE Mahendravarman I

    **630–668** CE Narasimhavarman I

    **695–728** CE Rajasimha (Narasimhavarman II)

    **731–796** CE Nandivarman II

    **846–869** CE Nandivarman III

Hindu revival and bhakti movement. Maritime invasion of Sri Lanka in 668 CE, the first of many Tamil invasions of Sri Lanka.

Protracted warfare during the rule of Mahendravarman and Narasimhavarman with the Chalukyas of Badami and Pulakesin II.

**543–755** CE Chalukyas of Badami.

**606–647** CE Harshavardhana, emperor of Kanauj.

**630–643** CE Hieun Tsang, Buddhist pilgrim from China, visited India.

**7th century** CE Hindu kingdoms of South-East Asia—Myanmar, Malay Peninsula, Sri Vijaya (Palembang in Sumatra), Java and Borneo.

**8th century** CE Sailendra kings overthrew the Hindu kingdom of Sri Vijaya and established a vast kingdom from Java to Sumatra to Kedah in the Malay Peninsula.

**8th century – 10th century** CE Rashtrakutas ruled over the Deccan. Northern India under the Gurjara Pratiharas and Palas.

**850–1279** CE The age of the Cholas. Major Chola emperors:

      **985–1016** CE Rajaraja I

      **1012–1044** CE Rajendra I

      **1070–1122** CE Kulottunga I

      **1118–1135** CE Vikrama Chola

      **1133–1150** CE Kulottunga II

Period of territorial expansion. The Chola empire further consolidated when Kulottunga I, grandson of Rajendra I and descendant of the eastern Chalukyas, became the king, uniting the Chola and eastern Chalukya kingdoms.

Political and administrative development and strengthening of local bodies. Many large temples and temple complexes erected which became physical landmarks and central social institutions under the Cholas.

**993–1073 CE** Cholas followed an aggressive policy of maritime conquest and invaded Sri Lanka many times:

> **993 CE** Invasion of Sri Lanka by Rajaraja I.
>
> **1017–18 CE** Conquest of Sri Lanka by Rajendra I. Sri Lanka became a province of the Chola empire. Invasions also by Rajendra's successors.
>
> **1073 CE** Vijayabahu became king of Sri Lanka overthrowing Chola occupation.

**1025 CE** Sea expedition and the conquest of Kadaram and Sri Vijaya by Rajendra Chola.

**c. 1100 CE** Construction of the temple of Angkor Wat in Kambuja.

**1000–1026 CE** Invasions of north India by Mahmud of Ghazni.

**c. 1200 CE** Establishment of the Delhi sultanate.

# PROLOGUE

## A HISTORICAL BACKGROUND[1]

PRIOR TO EVEN its recorded history, the Tamil region or Tamilakam had a well-defined cultural and linguistic identity. In the third century BCE, Kautilya alluded to the potential for trade with south India and enumerated the many products of the region in the *Arthasastra*. The rock-cut edicts of Emperor Asoka mentioned the rulers of Tamilakam as Chola, Pandya, Keralaputra and Satiyaputra, in other words, the Chola, Pandya and Chera kings. After the Mauryas, the Deccan was ruled by the Satavahanas from the first century to the third century CE, and their empire extended into north India also. In 78 CE, Kanishka became the Kushana emperor, marking the beginning of the Saka era. In contrast to these empires, the Tamil region did not witness the rise of great kingdoms until much later.

The period from the first to the third century CE is generally referred to as the Sangam age in Tamil history. Tamilakam derived its name and identity not from the kings who ruled the territory, but from the Tamil language, which gave cohesion and unity to the region. The term Sangam pertains to the school of Tamil poetry and literature which was situated at Madurai. However, only manuscripts relating to the last or third Sangam are available to us at present. Tamilakam was ruled by the 'three kings' or *muvendar*. The Pandyas had their capital at Madurai, the Cholas at Uraiyur (Tiruchi) and the Cheras at Vanji (Karur). There were also many other minor principalities whose rulers were often referred to as *velir*. Though a few kings are named in the poems, we are unable to trace the genealogy of any particular king or dynasty during this period. Despite intermittent wars, the first century was a golden era for trade, especially with imperial Rome, until Emperor Vespasian in 75 CE decided to curb trade with Tamilakam and other parts of India in order to reduce the drain of precious metals from Rome. The Sangam poems however indicate an equally vibrant seaborne commerce with countries in South-East Asia. The anonymous work *Periplus of the Erythrean Sea*, dating to about 75 CE, gives an authoritative and first-hand account of seaports and commerce on the west and east coasts of India.

However, during the period from 300 to 550 CE there are virtually no sources available for a study of the history of the Tamil region and the period was described as 'a long historical night'. Little is known about this period, though it is referred to as the 'Kalabhra interregnum', an era when the region was under the control of Buddhist invaders, portrayed in Tamil literature as evil interlopers. Jainism and Buddhism took root in the Tamil region during this period. It was not a wholly dark stage in history as the Tamil epics *Silappadikaram* and *Manimekalai* were written in this period,[2] as was the *Tirukkural*, the great Tamil work on ethics. The *Silappadikaram* clearly reflects Jain influence, and the *Manimekalai* is deeply rooted in Buddhism. The *Tirukkural* does not disclose a religious bias but its author, Tiruvalluvar, is believed to have belonged to the Jain faith. In contrast to this period of 'historical night', in these centuries, north India was ruled by the Guptas who controlled a great and powerful empire.

At the beginning of the fifth century, Hindu kings began to rule in South-East Asia in the kingdoms of Kambuja (Cambodia) and Champa (Vietnam). In the seventh century, Hindu kingdoms existed in Burma and the Malay Peninsula as also in Sri Vijaya (Palembang) in Sumatra, Java (Savakam in Tamil) and Borneo.

The period from the middle of the sixth century to

the mid tenth century marked a revival in the Tamil region in more sense than one. The Kalabhras were defeated and great kingdoms ruled by powerful dynasties arose in Tamilakam, beginning with the Pallavas in northern Tamilakam. Simhavishnu (556–89 CE) was the first of the great Pallava kings, followed by his son Mahendravarman (590–629 CE) and his grandson Narasimhavarman I (630–68 CE). The reign of Mahendravarman witnessed the revival of Hinduism in the south, and is popularly attributed to the great Saivite saint Tirunavukkarasar. A period of strong Hindu revival commonly referred to as the bhakti movement followed when Saivite and Vaishnavite saints produced a voluminous body of devotional, esoteric poetry of great lyrical beauty, namely *Tevaram* and *Nalayira Divya Prabandam*. The first naval invasion of Sri Lanka was undertaken in 668 CE by Narasimhavarman I to restore the Sinhala prince Manavarman to the throne in the island kingdom. Other great Pallava kings were Rajasimha (690–728/9 CE), Nandivarman II (731–96 CE) and Nandivarman III (846–69 CE). Incidentally, Nandivarman II was elected to the throne as a boy when the direct line of the Pallava kings died out.

Further south, the Pandya kingdom was also gathering strength. These four centuries of political consolidation in north and south Tamilakam also witnessed many battles between the Pallavas and Pandyas who were engaged in a long-drawn-out struggle for supremacy in the region.

In the north-west, the Chalukyas of Badami controlled a vast empire, while Emperor Harshavardhana ruled over another empire from his capital at Kanauj. The Pallavas and Chalukyas invaded each other's kingdoms and fought many battles, of which perhaps the best known was the invasion of Vatapi by Narasimhavarman I, when the Chalukya king Pulakesin II was killed.

Buddhist pilgrims from China such as Hieun Tsang also travelled to India during the seventh century to visit religious centres in India and left detailed chronicles of their journeys in India. This was therefore a period of close cultural exchange with China. Towards the end of the rule of the T'ang dynasty (c. 900), China's overland and overseas contacts with India and other countries came to an end and were not revived until the Song dynasty came to power.

In the eighth century, the Hindu kingdom of Sri Vijaya was overthrown by the powerful empire of the Sailendras stretching from Java, Sumatra to the Malay Peninsula (Kedah or Kadaram), and became the most extensive and powerful kingdom in South-East Asia.

From 750 to 900 CE the Deccan was ruled by the Rashtrakutas. Further north, there were several strong kingdoms like the Palas, Gurjara Pratiharas, Chandelas and others, but none matched the grandeur of Harshavardhana's great empire.

The four centuries spanning 850 to 1279 CE saw the rise of the Cholas whose empire was arguably the greatest of the kingdoms of Tamilakam. The Cholas had been completely marginalized by the Pallavas and Pandyas after the sixth century, but gradually regained their power in the ninth century beginning with Vijayalaya (850–71 CE), the founder of this dynasty. The greatest kings of the line were Rajaraja I (985–1016 CE) and his son Rajendra I (1012–44 CE). Both stretched the boundaries of their kingdom by military conquest, and Rajendra's armies went up north as far as the river Ganga, earning him the sobriquet of Gangaikondacholan. Both also followed an aggressive maritime policy, invading Sri Lanka in 993 CE and 1017–18 CE, incorporating Sri Lanka as a province of the Chola empire. The Sri Lankan king Vijayabahu however regained the kingdom and declared his independence in 1073 CE. The other major Chola emperors were Kulottunga I (1070–1122 CE), Vikrama Chola (1118–35 CE) and Kulottunga II (1133–50 CE). By the middle of the twelfth century, Chola power was definitely on the wane, but the empire survived for another century, till 1279 CE.

Many changes in governance were introduced under the Cholas in terms of tax administration and reorganization of revenue regions and local corporate institutions. Construction of huge temples and temple complexes which dominated the physical landscape and social life of the region was an important part of Chola imperial rule. Perhaps the most famous of these was the temple built by Rajaraja I at Tanjavur, known as Rajarajesvaram, or simply the 'big temple', which was consecrated in 1010 CE. The Hindu kingdoms of South-East Asia continued without major interruptions till the end of Chola rule and even later. The famous temple of Angkor Wat in Cambodia was built at the beginning of the twelfth century.

In contrast to the Tamil region where there was a long spell of political stability and continuity, north India witnessed many upheavals from the beginning of the eleventh century, notably the repeated invasions by Mahmud of Ghazni.

The Delhi sultanate was established towards the end of the twelfth century ushering in many centuries of Muhammadan rule.

# 1. MERCHANTS AND TRADE IN THE PRE-MODERN ERA: ISSUES AND INSIGHTS

DOWN THE CENTURIES, from times immemorial, the Indian Ocean had been at the centre of global maritime trade, both literally and figuratively, and was the conduit that linked the known world from the Mediterranean in the west to the South China Sea in the east. The Indian Ocean region extended from the west coast of Africa to South-East Asia, comprising a myriad of communities, religions and cultures. The ports on the east and west coasts of India, strategically located in the geographic centre of this region, became entrepôts of commercial exchange and of cultural diffusion since merchant ships from the west rarely sailed further east beyond the Bay of Bengal, while the ships from the east, especially China, did not venture further west than the ports of Kerala.

The graph contours of trade in the Indian Ocean survived with great stability over many centuries even after European nations had penetrated this trade circuit. Maritime trade, however, was only one part of the extended chain of trade which integrated regional and supra-local markets with ports and overseas markets, and merchants were the prime movers in this economic scenario.

## Issues and insights

The nature of trade and merchant activity in the pre-medieval period gives rise to a number of questions and insights into historical institutional processes. At the most basic level, trading as a specialized activity carried on by a distinctive class of merchants implicitly indicates a diversified economy which has expanded beyond subsistence; this holds true for production and consumption too. Production, even of primary goods like food grains, was oriented to non-local markets. Equally, trade promoted the production of a diverse range of manufactured goods for the market which resulted in the development of skills, basic technology and specialization. Consumption also expanded beyond what was produced or available locally. In short, trade became the engine of growth in the pre-modern world before the rise of industrial capitalism.

Risk was a factor of overriding importance in pre-modern trade. Mercantile organizations and institutions were primarily oriented to negotiating the risks involved in trade. There were two aspects to the risk factor. The first were the physical dangers of long-distance trade over land or sea. In overland trade, merchants constantly faced the dangers of unsafe roads and lack of security since the authority of the pre-medieval state rarely extended to remote areas, and overland trade routes could not be patrolled to provide safe passage to travellers. Overseas trade involved not merely the dangers of long sea voyages in primitive ships, but also necessitated prolonged stay in foreign ports for the merchants. The second aspect of the risk related to the paucity of information due to virtually non-existent communication technology. Merchants operated with minimal and mostly unreliable information about distant markets which had to be factored into their decisions on what and how much to buy and where and when to sell.

Seafaring in the pre-modern period, especially in the Indian Ocean, was driven by the pattern of monsoon winds and voyages had to be undertaken according to the seasonal winds. This imposed many limitations on travel and merchants perforce had to spend long periods residing in foreign ports to conduct their transactions before being able to return to their native places, resulting in the rise of trade diaspora in international ports. This pattern, in fact, was prevalent even up to the eighteenth century. Often, such merchant groups tended to become immigrant communities, living in enclaves in different ports. This led to two possible behavioural outcomes. First, there was a fierce determination among each group to retain its cultural identity and individuality. Second, there was a tendency for cultural and social integration with the host society that led to the diffusion of religion and culture across many countries. In fact, the host societies also evinced the need to isolate foreign merchant communities to retain their own identity.[1] Evidence of such ethnic isolation and cultural diffusion is seen even now in the large numbers of Chinese communities in most ports in South-East Asia, the strong presence of Islam on the south-west coast of India and in Indonesia, the Hindu temples of Angkor in Cambodia, and the continuing influence of the Hindu epics *Ramayana* and *Mahabharata* and Sanskritized names even in the Islamic or Buddhist societies of South-East Asia. These cross-cultural interactions were important markers in mercantile history over the centuries.

Another determining factor is the role of the state in promoting trade. The state did not always suggest the presence of a strong, centralized authority. Institutions of the state included local bodies, corporate assemblies and regional authorities. The functioning of these institutions and their intervention in trade and mercantile activity needs to be explored as another facet of the conditions under which trade operated in pre-modern times.

Finally, we need to look at questions about merchants who were the main protagonists in pre-modern economies. What were the spheres of activity and interactions between functionally differentiated classes of merchants? What were their links to maritime trade? Did they own the ships used in coastal and maritime trade? Did their activities conform to the 'peddler' model of pre-modern intra-Asian trade?[2] The objective of this monograph is to study these issues as well as the complex dynamics of trade which flourished despite primitive technologies in production, transportation and communication in the ancient and medieval period with special reference to the Tamil merchants, state and society.

## Tamil merchants and trade: A synopsis

Historical reconstruction of the past essentially depends on the sources available. For the ancient period, sources present two kinds of problems, namely of the scarcity of data and the reliability of information. In the case of the

Tamil country or Tamilakam, a rich corpus of literary works written in the early centuries of the Common Era during the Sangam period[3] constitutes the main source. The use of literary sources is fraught with many pitfalls. To begin with, there is no chronological sequence or continuity in the sources. In using these sources we also have to make a judgement call on whether the poet was describing the reality of what he experienced or whether he was painting an idealized picture of the real world or whether the works pertained to any basic reality at all. Subject to these caveats, it can be said that the descriptions of ports, cities, trade and merchants in the *Pattupattu*, The Ten Songs, of the Sangam period, and the two epics *Silappadikaram* and *Manimekalai* of a somewhat later period have a vitality and vividness which lend themselves to historical analysis. Archaeological finds, especially of Roman coins and artefacts in many ports and inland areas of Tamilakam, support the information contained in the literary sources about the extent of trade with the Mediterranean region in the ancient period. The limited number of scattered inscriptions in Tamil Brahmi script is also useful as corroborative material. The source materials for this period are further enriched by the accounts of contemporary geographers of Rome and Alexandria like Strabo, Pliny and Ptolemy, in addition to *Periplus of the Erythrean Sea*, the first-hand anonymous account written in 75 CE.

For the early medieval period of the Pallava and Chola empires, inscriptions constitute the main source. Here there is no problem of volume or reliability. The published inscriptions alone run to tens of thousands. The challenge is to integrate the scattered information into meaningful analytical categories for understanding mercantile activity, behaviour and institutions.

In the ultimate analysis, we can derive a great deal of information which helps us to understand the nature of Tamil merchants and trade during the ancient and early modern periods. However, many questions remain unanswered, which means that our understanding can only be partial and our quest incomplete in some respects.

Chapter 2 gives an account of merchants and trade in Tamilakam in the Sangam era. During this period the region was ruled by several chieftains or petty kings, in spite of the exaggerated references to the three great kingdoms of the Pandya, Chola and Chera. The fragmented political landscape was also subject to a high degree of instability because of frequent local wars. Despite this, we find that the region supported an extended seaborne trade from the Mediterranean to South-East Asia. A strong state was therefore not a prerequisite for mercantile activities to flourish as long as the latter were allowed to function freely without extortionate taxation, controls or other state intervention. The evidence suggests that in Tamilakam merchants were not a homogeneous group or class. Different classes of merchants trading in diverse markets and goods, ranging from craftsmen who peddled their own products to maritime merchants, integrated a hierarchy of markets from the local to the regional to the external and overseas markets. The goods traded covered a vast range of utility and luxury products from food grains and pepper to cloth, aromatic substances and precious gems like corals and pearls, which would seem effectively to counter the model which characterized Asian trade as 'peddling trade' restricted to inconsequential luxuries.

Chapter 3 gives a brief account of the rise of the major kingdoms of Tamilakam—the Pallavas based in Kanchipuram and later the extensive and strong Chola kingdom based in Tanjavur. The rise of these kingdoms stabilized the political scenario of the region and provided a well-ordered and institutionalized administrative machinery in Tamilakam. The development of strong local corporate bodies to manage local resources and the rise of temples as a major social institution were the two major developments in the history of early medieval Tamilakam which had a direct impact on the economy, especially on merchants, trade and mercantile institutions. This period also saw the Tamil kings engaging with the kingdoms of South-East Asia and Sri Lanka in a significant manner.

Chapter 4 examines the institutions of the *nagaram*, a 'corporate assembly of merchants', and the guild in relation to the synergy provided by temples as the major integrative institution in Tamil society, in addition to the activities and trade conducted by the merchants as individuals. As noted, the lack of a cohesive political structure or strong, centralized kingdoms did not necessarily negatively impact trade and commerce. However, the existence of a centralized and powerful state and political stability led to the evolution of strong institutional structures which led to greater levels of commercial activity, and paved the way for the rise of a more modern economy of merchant capitalists and commercial institutions.

Chapter 5 brings together all these insights into an overview of the Tamil merchants and trade over one thousand years.

# 2. TRADE AND MERCHANTS IN ANCIENT TAMILAKAM

## TAMILAKAM: AN INTRODUCTION

THE TAMIL REGION of India, situated strategically in the Indian Ocean between South-East and West Asia, has a long history of trade going back more than two millennia. But what exactly did the term Tamilakam, or Tamil region, denote? According to the Tamil epic *Silappadikaram*:[1]

> The Tamil region extends from the hills of Vishnu [Tirupati] in the north to the oceans at the cape in the south. In this region of cool waters were the four great cities of Madurai with its towers; Uraiyur which was famous; tumultuous Kanchi; and Puhar with the roaring waters [of the river Kaveri and the ocean].

Geographically, therefore, the Tamil region denoted peninsular India south of the Deccan plateau, extending from the Bay of Bengal in the east to the Arabian Sea in the west.

The notion of Tamilakam was based on a larger linguistic and cultural identity and did not denote a single political identity or nation state. Traditionally, the Tamil region was said to be ruled by *muvendar*, the three kings: Pandya, Chola and Chera. Madurai, Uraiyur, which is now a suburb of Tiruchi, and Vanji (modern Karur)² were the respective capitals of the three kingdoms. To these should be added the kingdom in the north, with its capital in Kanchi or Kanchipuram, which was later ruled by the Pallavas. In addition to the capital cities, many ports along the eastern coast are mentioned in Sangam literature. Foremost among them was Puhar, also known an Pumpuhar or Kaveri(pum)pattinam, situated at the mouth of one of the distributaries of the Kaveri and the sea, north of Nagapattinam, which was often described as *managaram*, the great city. Many other ports are also mentioned in Sangam poems. In addition, archaeological evidence has established that Arikamedu or Virampatnam, just south of Pondicherry, and Alagankulam near Rameswaram, though it is no longer on the sea, were ports visited by Roman traders.³ The ports more frequently mentioned in foreign accounts were on the west coast. Musiri or Muziris was the major port of the

Chera kingdom (modern Kodungallur, earlier known as Cranganore)[4] from where pepper was exported. Further to the north was the port of Tyndys or Tondi (now known as Ponnani), not to be confused with the port of the same name on the east coast in the Pandyan kingdom.

In spite of the poetic hyperbole about the three 'kings' and their extended authority, in reality, during the ancient period, the 'kingdoms' were principalities ruled by warring chieftains.[5] Such smaller political units were constantly looking to augment their resource base, necessitated by the narrow limits of their territorial authority. Frequent military campaigns and conquests of territory, especially from the *velir*, petty chieftains, were thus a feature of the political history of the region. Thus, in Sangam poetry, the warrior king was the metaphor for a great king of heroic qualities and for great kingship. Neduncheliyan, the Pandya king; Tirumavalavan, the Chola king; Senguttuvan, the Chera king; and Ilantiraiyan, the ruler of Kanchi[6] as well as minor chieftains are all eulogized for their great qualities as leaders of their armies and for their conquests.

Notwithstanding the instability inherent in this fragmented political landscape and the frequent occurrences of military conflict in the region, there seems to have been no significant or noticeable disruption of trade in the region, either in internal or in coastal trade. Literary works confirm this. Our reconstruction of external trade is further substantiated by stronger evidence from archaeological data and contemporary foreign accounts. The resilience of trade independent of political stability was a remarkable feature of ancient Tamilakam.

## TRADE AND MANUFACTURE

Trade was recognized as the engine of growth and economic well-being in Tamilakam. Old texts listed six pre-eminent economic activities—cultivation, manufacturing, trade, pictorial art, learning and sculpture. This list also gives an insight into the cultural priorities and the ambience of the region. However, the consensus among most commentators and scholars was that cultivation and trade were the two most important economic activities,[7] and certainly the most significant in terms of volume. Contemporary poets, for instance, referred to persons who had grown rich on cultivation and trade.[8] Linking agriculture with commerce also indicates that the surplus generated in agriculture, the largest sector, was mobilized through trade, providing the much-needed capital resources for commercial activities.[9] Nevertheless, more advanced levels of trade coexisted with a large and extensive subsistence economy in Tamilakam. Only the former lends itself to analysis, however, especially because of its potential to trigger sustained economic growth.

## Ports and maritime trade: The literary evidence

Maritime trade contributed in a visible and significant manner to the total trade of ancient Tamilakam. This is reflected in the vivid descriptions of trade and shipping in Sangam literature, which often mentioned the ships of the *yavana* or merchants from Rome. These ships brought commodities from Rome which were exchanged for pepper and other products of the Tamil region. 'Well-built yavana ships came with gold to prosperous Musiri and left with pepper.' These ships also brought to the Pandyan kingdom 'cool scented wine' which was much desired by the people and made them happy.[10]

Ports were naturally major trade centres where all the circuits of trade—overseas, overland and coastal— converged, and where people of varied nationalities speaking diverse languages met. Most of the ports described in Sangam literature were on the east coast of Tamilakam.[11] In the Pandya kingdom, Korkai was the southernmost port, situated in the Gulf of Mannar. It was the centre of pearl fishing, where the oysters had pearls as large as teeth.[12] To the north, also in the Gulf of Mannar, was Saliyur, where:

> Clouds hang over the sea; the wind sounds like drums; ships with flags sail into the harbour bringing fine goods like gold which are used by everyone. Over the harbour the lowering clouds look like mountains. Saliyur, which had the same name as a fine variety of rice, and was encircled by the ocean as its moat, was conquered by Neduncheliyan.[13]

The same poem also noted that all along the coast in the Pandya kingdom:

> People who sail their ships across the oceans come together and sell the horses they bring in exchange for the goods brought by coastal ships. The Pandya kingdom had many prosperous coastal towns with boats carrying fine pearls, conch bangles, many varieties of grain, white salt, tamarind and dried fish, and their number increased day by day.[14]

The port of Tondi was in the Palk Strait to the north of Rameswaram.[15]

> At Tondi, merchants bring eaglewood, cloth, sandalwood, camphor and other fragrant substances in their ships across the wide seas. The eastern air [blowing] from Tondi brings these scents to Madurai, the city of the Pandyan.[16]

Judging by the number of ports in the Gulf of Mannar and Palk Straits which are mentioned in Sangam poetry, it can be inferred that in the ancient period ships were able to sail along the west coast of Sri Lanka since they were smaller, whereas even in the seventeenth century ships were larger and had to sail around the eastern coast of Sri Lanka.

The most important port on the east coast undoubtedly was Puhar, which was described in great detail in *Pattinappalai* and *Silappadikaram*.

> Puhar is of undying fame, protected by the gods. It is filled with horses brought in ships; sacks of pepper brought on carts; gemstones and gold from the northern mountains; sandalwood and eaglewood from the western hills; pearls from the southern seas; coral from the eastern seas; wheat from the Gangetic region, rice from the Kaveri plains; food from Sri Lanka and gold from Kadaram.[17] Puhar has broad streets piled with rare and expensive goods.
>
> In Puhar, boats are anchored along the shore like a row of tethered horses. They come with rice which is exchanged for the price of white salt . . . In the harbour, the anchored ships with flags on the masts resembled tethered elephants.[18]
>
> In this town lived many merchants who brought in wonderful and expensive goods from other

countries across the seas on large ships and overland on carts and carried on their trade here . . . . Along the seafront was the beautiful sight of heaps of goods; and of anchored ships with their cargo.[19]

Further north were the ports of Eyirpattinam, which had a fort wall and where eaglewood was brought by sea,[20] and Pattinappakkam, where ships came from the north with horses with milk-white manes and other consumption goods.[21]

These descriptions provide valuable insights into the patterns of trade. There was a flourishing trade in food grains, and urban markets had a special street devoted to the sale of food grains, of which there were 'eight, sixteen or eighteen varieties of grains'. In addition to what was locally produced, food grains were also imported. The commodities brought through land routes from the interior to the coast were primarily pepper, eaglewood, sandalwood and gemstones, while salt was the main product carried from the coast to the interior. The patterns of trade were also indicative of the natural products of the different eco-zones of the Tamil region. A distinctive feature of Sangam poetry was the classification of these zones under five *tinais*— *neydal* or coastal, *marudam* or cultivated plains, *palai* or desert, *mullai* or pastoral, and *kurinji*, the hills. While these tinais were primarily used by poets to evoke different moods, they also reflected the nature of economic activity and the products that characterized each zone. Thus salt and other marine products like pearls and fish came from the coast, while the hills produced aromatic woods and pepper. Food grains were grown in the cultivated plains, and all these products were exchanged extensively in internal trade.

Goods brought in by sea to the ports were also distributed in the hinterland through overland trade. Coastal trade was important, and mostly involved the import of food grains from further north along the Bay of Bengal, which were exchanged for white salt, a pattern of coastal trade that continued to be important even down to the nineteenth century. Pearls, dried fish, tamarind and conch-shell bangles were also shipped by small coastal craft which plied up and down the coast. There was a great deal of shipping activity in the Bay of Bengal. According to the *Periplus of the Erythrean Sea*, in the first century CE, three types of vessels were found in these waters—country ships trading along the coast; large vessels made of single logs bound together, called *sangara*; and the very large ships called *colandia* which made the voyage to Malaya and north to the Ganga.[22]

There was a very high level of demand for aromatic products. Though eaglewood and sandalwood were both grown in the western hills, the supply was inadequate

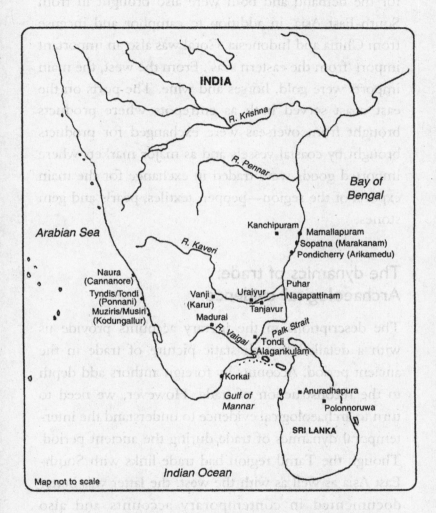

**Map 2.1 Capital Cities and Ports of Tamilakam: Sangam Period**

for the demand and both were also brought in from South-East Asia, in addition to camphor and incense from China and Indonesia. Coral was also an important import 'from the eastern seas'. From the west, the main imports were gold, horses and wine. The ports on the east coast served both as entrepôts where products brought from overseas were exchanged for products brought by coastal vessels and as major markets where imported goods were traded in exchange for the main exports of the region—pepper, textiles, pearls and gem stones.

## The dynamics of trade: Archaeological evidence

The descriptions in the literary accounts provide us with a detailed though static picture of trade in the ancient period. Accounts by foreign authors add depth to the reconstruction of trade. However, we need to turn to archaeological evidence to understand the inter-temporal dynamics of trade during the ancient period. Though the Tamil region had trade links with South-East Asia as well as with the west, the latter was better documented in contemporary accounts and also corroborated by archaeological evidence. Schoff noted that trade had been carried on between Egypt and India which extended to the Mediterranean region even in the pre-Roman period. The sea trade was controlled by the Arabs and Phoenicians and 'the cloths and precious stones, the timbers and spices . . . particularly cinnamon . . . were redistributed at Socotra or Guardafi, and carried to the Nile and Mediterranean'. Even after Rome had replaced Alexandria as the centre of Mediterranean trade, Arabs still controlled the sea trade and protected their monopoly by making sure that their knowledge of the patterns of the monsoon winds and information about the direct sea route to India and about products traded remained their secret. Arab traders retained their knowledge monopoly about the source markets in India for cinnamon, the commodity which had made their fortunes, even after Roman ships began to sail directly to India. [23]

The dynamics of trade between India and the Mediterranean changed due to many factors. Rome became the central power in the west and was the largest market for products from India. In the first century CE, Hippalus, an Egyptian pilot, 'discovered' the pattern of monsoon winds and the direct sea route to the west coast of India, which had been known only to Arab seafarers till then. This shortened the tedious and long voyage hugging the coast and also nullified the danger from the pirates who preyed on vessels in the coastal waters. Rome, as a policy measure, avoided the overland routes through Parthia and encouraged direct sea trade with India. This resulted in a significant increase in the total volume of Roman ships from barely twenty ships a year to almost a ship a day.[24]

The increased volume of shipping reflected the growth in demand in Rome for commodities from India. Since the value of exports from Rome was much lower than the value of goods imported, the trade imbalance was made up in specie. Pliny, writing in 75 CE, complained that there was 'no year in which India does not drain our Empire of at least fifty five million sesterces'.[25] In fact, trade with Rome peaked in the latter half of the first century CE during the reign of Tiberius, which is substantiated by the large share of the coins of Augustus and Tiberius among all the Roman coins found in India.[26]

Tamilakam had been trading with Rome even when Rome was a republic. Roman artefacts, including coins of the Roman republic which have been dated to the third century BCE, have been excavated in Arikamedu, near Pondicherry, which was an 'Indo-Roman trading station',[27] and these establish conclusively the antiquity of the trade with Rome.

Roman ships did not sail beyond Cape Comorin until the early decades of the first century CE. Pliny's account which depended on earlier authors for information on India mentioned no ports beyond the west coast.[28] During this period Roman traders travelled overland from the west coast through the Palghat pass to market centres in the east via Coimbatore, Erode and Karur. These districts were on the main trade routes linking the east coast with the west and served as major market centres. Besides, pepper and cardamom, the major exports, were grown in the western region. Beryl, a highly prized gem stone much in demand in Rome, came from mines in Kodumanal and Padiyur in Erode and Vaniyampadi near Salem. Excavations have also established that Chennimalai in Erode was a major centre for the production of iron and steel which were probably exported to Rome.[29] Remnants of furnaces and slag have been found in Chennimalai and Karur. All this explains why the finds of earlier Roman coins are concentrated in the districts of Coimbatore, Erode, Salem and Karur.[30]

By the second half of the first century CE, Roman ships had begun to sail directly to ports on the east coast. *Periplus of the Erythrean Sea* was written at the same time as Pliny's account, and is the factual firsthand account of a person who actually sailed to India and traded there. The *Periplus* describes ports on the west and east coasts, showing that Roman traders had begun to access the eastern ports by sea. Ptolemy's *Geography*, written around 125 CE, lists ports on the Coromandel coast and also further east, an indication of the growing state of knowledge in the west about regions further east in Asia.[31]

According to the *Periplus*, the ports of Naura or Cannanore and Tyndys or Tondi were at the northern border of Tamilakam ('Damirica') and were ports in the Chera kingdom. To the south, Musiri also in the Chera kingdom, was an important port which 'abounds in ships sent . . . from Arabia and the Greeks'. Nelcynda, near Kottayam, further south, was in the Pandyan kingdom.[32] Large ships from the west came to these ports because of the vast quantities of pepper and malabathrum, the leaf of the cinnamon tree used as an aromatic, available there. Goods brought in by these ships included large quantities of coins, topaz, antimony, coral, crude glass, copper, tin and lead, some wine and a small quantity of textiles. The ships took back pepper, vast amount of pearls, ivory, silk cloth, spikenard, a fragrant ointment or oil from the Gangetic region, malabathrum from the interior, transparent stones, evidently beryls, diamonds, sapphire and tortoiseshell.[33] Tortoiseshell was brought to Musiri from islands near Malaya, and Schoff comments that this reference gave an accurate insight into the brisk trade of south India with South-East Asia.[34] This list of the exports from Rome and imports into Rome from Tamilakam clearly exemplifies the adverse trade balance of Rome due to the high value of the luxury goods imported from India, which had to be made up by the export of silver and gold coins.

A recently discovered papyrus, now in the Vienna Museum, dating to the second century CE, has a contract written in Greek between a merchant of Musiri and a merchant of Alexandria with respect to a shipment from Musiri. One side records a business loan drawn up in Musiri. The other side, written in Alexandria, lists the imports from Musiri—spikenard, ivory and bales of cloth. 'The business contract . . . covers the period of shipment from Muziris until the arrival of the cargo at Alexandria and mentions the specific type of merchandise, the quantity and value as well as the 25 percent tax rate levied by Roman customs officials.'[35] The cargo amounted to 700 to 1700 pounds of spikenard, 4700 pounds of ivory items, and 790 pounds of varieties of textiles. The total value of this cargo was equal to the price of 2400 acres of land in Egypt.[36] The document clearly shows that individual merchant exporters operated on a large scale even in the ancient period. We can also see that trade in the ancient period was conducted over very long distances, either overland or

by sea. Spikenard was also known as Gangetic nard,
signifying that it came from the north of India, and yet
it was being exported from a port on the south-west
coast, situated diagonally across the country. Importantly,
it gives an insight into the modalities of business
arrangements in the ancient period. There were written
contracts, covering the duration of the voyage and
specifying the quantities and value of the goods traded.
The reference to the business loan shows that long-
term credit arrangements were in place and were used
to enable the smooth functioning of trade.

Musiri, as we have seen, was also mentioned in Sangam
literature and a poet said that at Musiri fish was bartered
for rice brought in baskets; sacks of pepper were brought
to the market from the houses; and the gold which
came in the ships in exchange for the goods sold was
brought on barges to the shore.[37]

On the east coast, the *Periplus* noted, the important
ports were Korkai, with the pearl fisheries. Further
north and inland was the region of Uraiyur, 'Argaru',
where all the pearls gathered on the coast were brought.
From here came the muslins known as 'Argaritic' which
were sent to Rome. The other ports on the Coromandel
Coast mentioned in the *Periplus* have been identified as
Puhar, Puducheri or Pondicherry and Sopatna.[38] The
Tamil region, and especially the Chola kingdom, already

had a thriving weaving industry and was famous for cotton textiles which were exported. Arikamedu and Alagankulam, near Rameswaram were also ports where Roman ships came to trade. While the archaeological finds of Arikamedu are widely known, the beautiful graffito of a Roman ship on a piece of pottery at Alagankulam is less well known, and is further proof that Roman ships regularly visited the eastern ports. The ship has been identified as a three-master Roman sailing ship of the first to third centuries CE, which was of the largest type of trading ships used on the long

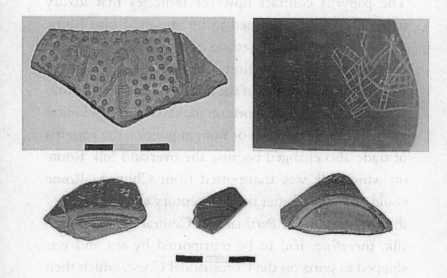

Figure 2.1 Alagankulam Potteries: Roman Influence
(Courtesy: Tamil Nadu State Department of Archaeology)

voyage to India.[39] These trading ports, Arikamedu, Alagankulam and Puhar, as well as the inland capital Madurai, had settled Roman colonies.[40]

The pattern of trade between Rome and India began to change after the civil war following the death of Nero in 68 CE. Emperor Vespasian passed a series of laws against the luxurious lifestyle of the upper classes, and imports from India began to be largely confined to pepper and textiles, both comparatively low-value commodities. Luxury items like silk, ivory and beryl began to be traded increasingly in intra-Asian trade.[41] The papyrus contract however indicates that luxury items like ivory continued to be imported into Rome from India even in the second century CE.

There was also a definite shift in the direction of Roman trade, and most of the trade after the first century CE was conducted with ports on the east coast. In addition to the internal problems of Roman politics, the patterns of trade also changed because the overland Silk Route on which silk was transported from China to Rome could not be used after the first century BCE as a result of the hostility of the Parthians in Central Asia. Chinese silk, therefore, had to be transported by sea and was shipped to ports on the Coromandel Coast, which then served as entrepôts from where the silk was shipped to Rome.[42]

The trade with South-East Asia and the commodities imported from there were often mentioned in Sangam literature. Trade links with China can only be deduced inferentially, from the references to the import of camphor and gold. Further, silk and silk yarn which was used in textile production must have been imported from China since the Tamil region did not produce any silk. If the references made by Pan Kou, an early Chinese writer, have been correctly interpreted, it would indicate that commercial intercourse between China and South India was already quite extensive in the second century BCE, and that the Chinese were well acquainted with the political and commercial conditions in India.[43]

How were market exchanges conducted and price/value determined in trade? Though it has been argued that '[t]here is no evidence for transactions based on exchange value' and that all trade was conducted only on the basis of barter,[44] this does not seem tenable considering the realities of the logistics of long-distance maritime trade. It would have been impossible for trade to function on such a scale unless goods were exchanged for money. The enormous quantity of Chera coins that have been found on the bed of the river Amaravati in Karur also shows that money was definitely used as a medium of exchange. The finds ranged from copper coins dating to the second century BCE to silver portrait coins of the third century CE.[45]

Roman coins were also in circulation in addition to local coins. Many Roman coins have a small countermark (dots, crescents, circles and even Roman letters). Slashed Roman coins have also been found, and though many theories have been offered no definitive conclusion is possible to explain why these marks were made. However, countermarked coins seem to have been stamped thus so that they could circulate as legally accepted money. Such countermarks would also serve the purpose of identifying the owner of the coins which were deposited with moneylenders, indicating that some form of banking services existed in the ancient period. Many imitation Roman coins have also been discovered in many parts of India, arguably to be used in local circulation. There was no fraudulent or criminal intention behind minting these coins, and they equalled Roman coins in weight and purity of metal, and reveal a high degree of workmanship. These coins were probably made by an experienced Roman craftsman, or a skilled Indian craftsman trained by a Roman master.[46]

The question that remains unanswered is why these Roman coins were in circulation as legal tender at all. It is probable that, with the great expansion of maritime trade in the first century CE, the demand for money also increased which could not be met by the volume of local currency then available. Since the quality of Roman coins was accepted universally, they were used to supplement the money supply then in circulation. The increase in trade in the first century CE would have placed many pressures on the economic resources of Tamilakam. To increase production in response to the growing demand would require the augmentation of all productive resources—inputs, labour and capital. Cotton cloth was the major manufactured commodity exported. Increasing output by increasing productivity was not possible in the absence of technological development. Thus output could only be increased by employing more factors of production—more cotton, spinners, weavers and looms. In the long run, therefore, this implies an expansion of economic activity in the region which was reflected in the pressures on money supply. The indigenous economy evidently also had the flexibility necessary for accommodating itself to the changing direction of trade. The reduction in the volume of demand in Rome for luxury products was offset by the increase in trade with South-East Asia and the Far East.

## Manufactures

Contemporary literature indicates that many non-agricultural manufacturing activities were carried on in

Tamilakam. Textile production was the largest activity next to agriculture in terms of output. Textiles remained the most important commodity of export from India and, in fact, held up Indian manufacturing as the benchmark of excellence in global terms for nearly 2000 years. Weavers came from a community (later becoming a caste) known as Sali, and even today the Salis are predominant among the weaving castes in south India. Weavers lived in demarcated urban areas, and it can be said that the finer varieties of textiles used by the urban rich and for exports were woven by the urban weavers, whereas weavers in rural areas produced coarser cloth for local consumption. Many ancient texts noted that spinning of cotton yarn was done by women.[47] Spinning was a home-based occupation for women, and it remained so until the nineteenth century.

While the Salis wove the cloth, textiles were sold by merchants who specialized in the cloth trade, *aruvai vanikar*. In the cities there were demarcated streets for selling textiles, and the shops in Madurai had hundreds of scented saris stacked according to quality.[48] Weavers produced fine intricately designed silk and cotton fabrics, and wool from rat's hair, which was intended to give warmth.[49] Weaving of fine cloth was highly skilled work, and there are several references to the very thin, fine cloth woven with patterns. Such textiles were variously described as being so fine that the weave could not be discerned; as transparent and thin as snake skin; as fine as the vapour rising from milk. Fine cloth was kept scented with incense to keep it smelling fresh.[50]

Metal work was an important craft and there are many references to brass and copper smiths working in cities. Jewellery making and gold work were also major activities and the craftsmen who did this work were distinct from merchants who traded in gemstones and gold. The artisans who worked in these metals, along with blacksmiths and masons, were known as the 'five' *kammalar* or *kanmalar*, and these occupational castes were prominent in Tamil society till recent times. The demand for the products and services of these artisans was very high in cities and in Puhar 'craftsmen from Magadha, Maratta artisans, masons from Avanti and yavana carpenters' had worked on the royal pavilion along with local craftsmen.[51] A vivid picture of the variety of commodities that were available in cities is presented in the description of the main market of Madurai in *Silappadikaram*:

> The market streets were heaped with many expensive goods that would be desired even by kings: covered carts, two wheeled carts, beautiful chariots, armour to cover the entire body, elephant goads set with gems, armguards made of leather, waist bands, balls

of aromatic substances, white *chowris,* feather whisks, shields embossed with boar heads or forests, small leather shields, garlands made of pith, tools like saws, goods carved from ivory, scented paste and flower garlands.[52]

The patterns of consumption in urban society created a demand for the services of a great variety of craftsmen and skills which contributed to the diversification of the economy.

## Role of the state

It is difficult to define the role played by the state in promoting trade. On the positive side, the ruler, in this case the Pandyan king, was praised by the poet for 'increasing the wealth of the . . . people by procuring rare, valuable goods from various countries'. On the negative side, the military campaigns of the same king, Neduncheliyan, are listed, and the destruction caused by warfare and conquest is vividly described: 'fertile agricultural lands are burnt and devastated and have turned into forests; places where cattle used to be raised have become the haunts for tigers; and settlements have been ruined'.[53] Whether the net balance was beneficial or not is thus open to question.

It was recognized that one of the main obligations of

the state was to protect trade routes and traders from highway robbery and attacks. At least one poem in praise of Ilantiraiyan of Kanchi says that, in his country, there were no robbers who waylaid merchants and stole their goods because forest paths were guarded by soldiers with bows to protect merchants from attacks.[54] Nevertheless, the fact that merchants who travelled overland in groups were well armed to fight off robbers would indicate that such protection was minimal and that merchants depended on their own resources for security.

The state however was actively involved in collecting road tolls on goods carried overland[55] and customs duties on goods brought from overseas in the major ports. In Puhar:

> Near the seashore filled with flowering cactus are the men who collect customs duties which are due to a good king. They work untiringly like the sun collecting taxes ... This is the rare street of the customs booth. There the officials stamp goods with the seal of the tiger [the Chola emblem]. On these sacks of expensive goods, guard dogs with sharp nails roam and play with goats. Such is Puhar.[56]

At Puhar there was also a warehouse maintained by the government, which was known as *vellimadaimanram*.

Foreign merchants who came to Puhar had their goods stamped with their name, weight and measure and kept them in the warehouse. There were no guards at the entrance of the warehouse, nor were there doors with heavy bolts; nor did the owners of the goods guard their property. If anybody stole anything from the warehouse, they were made to walk around the city with the stolen goods on their heads and the goods were then confiscated. The warehouse made the people dread the thought of stealing.[57]

Since the epic refers also to 'the guards of the warehouse',[58] the earlier passage may be taken to be poetic exaggeration of the power of the state in curbing robbers.

In the final analysis, trade thrived in the region mainly due to the attitude of all the states which did not impede trade though they may not have actively promoted it either. Foreign merchants were welcome to come and trade in the ports and inland cities and were allowed to live peacefully and conduct their business. Cities and ports are always described as cosmopolitan centres where many languages were heard, and the fact that people of different countries were not discriminated against in any way created an atmosphere that was conducive to trade.

# MERCHANTS

In contrast to the data sources used in the account relating to trade in the ancient period, we rely almost exclusively on literary sources for a portrayal of merchants and mercantile activity. The use of literature as a historical source poses many problems, not the least of which is the subjective judgement of the researcher as to what extent the representation in the literary works represents reality and how much is idealized. Fortunately, contemporary inscriptions from the same period (around the beginning of the Common Era), though few in number, provide supplementary information which adds more texture to the account drawn from the literary works. In spite of this, many questions remain unanswered on mercantile organization and the economics of trade with respect to sources of capital, the nature and requirements of credit, or even the extent of monetization. Some conclusions may be drawn inferentially but remain as hypotheses.

## Social moorings

Merchants were prominent on the social and economic scene in Tamilakam, and were very active, especially in urban settlements. They were clearly held in high esteem in local society, in sharp contrast to the attitudes in

cultures as far apart spatially and culturally as ancient
Greece or medieval Japan, where commerce was looked
down upon as a lowly occupation. In ancient Greece,
gains from warfare and plunder was the noble ideal,
while commerce was seen only in a negative light, and
the common view was that trade was better left to
foreigners like the Phoenicians.[59] Interestingly, although
warfare and military aggression were equally valorized
in Tamil culture, merchants were considered honoured
and honourable members of society. *Pattinappalai*, one
of the ten poems of the *Pattuppattu*, said of the merchants
of Puhar:

> The merchants of Puhar are as straightforward as the
> crosspiece of a yoke. They always speak the truth and
> are fair-minded, and fear ignominy. They value their
> goods and the goods of others by the same standard;
> they neither take too high a price for their goods, nor
> do they shortchange on what they sell. They openly
> state their profits on the various goods they handle.
> Such merchants have lived in Puhar for many years.[60]

Another poem, *Maduraikkanchi*, praised the merchants
of Madurai who were 'virtuous householders'.[61]

These idealized representations surely reflected the
positive attitude towards merchants which prevailed in
Tamil society, which was due in no small part to the

recognition that merchants, by making available a variety of goods not otherwise available locally, enabled higher levels of sophisticated consumption which contributed to an improved quality of life. 'Merchants provide goods from the mountains and the seas which are of use and in great demand and give great happiness to the people.'[62] In fact, the contribution of merchants who had earned wealth and enjoyed a good reputation was acknowledged even by kings. In Madurai, the king honoured such merchants with the title of *etti* and a golden flower in recognition of this honour.[63]

Furthermore, merchants were respected for their bravery and martial qualities, which were much admired in local culture.

> They are hardworking; they wear footwear and body cover; because of their skill they are able to evade the arrows of highway robbers and have no scars of wounds on their chests; at their side they have shining swords with handles of ivory; they carry daggers on their waists which look like snakes; they wear tight clothes; they are brave warriors who will not turn their backs but will attack robbers with spears which they carry like [the God] Murugan.[64]

The great respect for merchants as a community is evident in the *Silappadikaram*. The central characters of the epic, Kannagi and Kovalan, belonged to the leading merchant families of Puhar, and the tale begins with an announcement of their forthcoming marriage. Kannagi was the daughter of a merchant of the Manaykan family, who was 'as generous as rainfall'. Kovalan's father, who belonged to the merchant class known as Perunkudi, is described thus:

> A rich merchant lived in Puhar who was held in great esteem by the Chola King as a leader among the local people. He helped many people with the money he earned from many righteous activities. His name was Masattuvan, and he also had an honorific title of 'an elder with two fortunes'.[65]

The *Silappadikaram* also noted that the rich merchants of Puhar were of good, virtuous families, and made donations to many charities.[66] Rich merchants were held in esteem because of their generosity and their contributions to the local community. They also supported local festivals and cultural activities, which secured their place in local society. Charitable donations by merchants are also recorded in the early inscriptions. Of the corpus of 116 inscriptions in Tamil Brahmi script which was in use till the early centuries of the Common Era, six refer to donations by merchants— four in Alagarmalai, to the north of Madurai, and two in Pugalur in Karur district, dating from the first century BCE to the third century CE.[67] These donor merchants are variously described as dealers in cloth, grain, oil and salt and were unlikely to have ranked among the richest class of merchants. Yet, a part of their limited resources was devoted to charity. This was probably motivated by a complex mix of values, beliefs and self-interest. Donations to religious institutions, in this case Jain or Buddhist institutions, were believed to ensure spiritual merit. Additionally these earned recognition and legitimacy for the donor in local society, building social capital which aided them in their business.

Prosperous merchants also had a visible presence in the community because of their lavish lifestyles. The descriptions of merchants of Puhar and Madurai note that they lived in tall, multi-storey houses which had latticed windows to let in the breeze and open terraces. The houses were filled with expensive goods and artefacts worth crores and great quantities of food, where even the kites flying past would have liked to rest. Beautiful women dressed in fine clothes could be seen at the windows.[68]

Evidently a high level of literacy prevailed in Tamil society in the ancient period. Merchants were highly literate and many noted poets were from the mercantile classes. One of the best known among them was Sattanar, the author of the second great Tamil epic *Manimekalai*, who was a grain merchant. *Mullaippattu*, one of the ten poems of the *Pattuppattu*, was composed by Nampudanar, a gold merchant. Many other poets were also referred to as merchants dealing in cloth, provisions and gold.[69] Since they were referred to as 'merchants', it is probable that they combined their literary activities with trade. Poets came from other occupational backgrounds also. Nakkirar, another famous poet, was from a conch-cutting family,[70] and, according to Puranic works in Tamil, was said to have even taken on an angry Siva in a literary debate. Poets also came from such diverse professions as medical practitioners and goldsmiths. This leads to a strong inference that literacy was widespread in Tamilakam in the ancient period, and was probably at a much higher level than in later centuries. It is therefore not surprising that merchants who contributed to literature were held in great esteem in a culture which valued learning.

## Agents of economic growth

The term 'merchant' did not refer to a homogeneous group or class. While all people engaged in commerce were merchants, *vanikan*, they were, however, a highly differentiated group. At one end of the scale were the rich merchants operating in the ports and capital cities;

at the other end were the peddlers who sold their wares on the streets. The largest and probably the most representative class was the single-commodity merchants often mentioned in literary works as well as in inscriptions. While caste was not unknown in ancient Tamil society, class was probably a stronger marker of identity among merchants than caste.

Many literary works and commentaries classified rich merchants into three subgroups, according to their wealth, as *Ippar*, *Kavippar* and *Perunkudi*.

> If the Ippar, Kavippar and Perunkudi merchants stood
> under an umbrella, mounted respectively on an
> elephant, a bull or in their footwear, and all their
> wealth was piled around them, they would not be
> able to see anything over the piles.[71]

While Ippar and Kavippar were probably only lexical terms, Perunkudi merchants are referred to in the literary works. The father of Kovalan, the hero of *Silappadikaram*, was a Perunkudi merchant, and his family background was often mentioned to establish the Kovalan's high social status, for instance when Kannagi went to the Pandyan king to protest his unjustified execution.

The rich merchants dealt in goods imported from overseas, as well as in goods brought overland from the interior. The *Silappadikaram* noted that 'the great city of

Puhar was filled with many merchants who brought in rare and expensive goods from other countries over seas and over land in ships and carts and carried on their trade'.[72] This would indicate that the big merchants were also ship owners who were engaged in maritime trade, though it has been argued that there is no evidence that the Tamil people engaged directly in ship owning or maritime trade.[73] Although the *Periplus* refers to the ships in coastal and long-distance trade, this does not necessarily mean that the ships were owned by the Tamil merchants. This is an instance where the literary reference needs further exploration for well-authenticated historical information.

Trade on such a large scale would require a large reserve of capital and considerable business skills. But there is no information as to how this was managed. What was the resource base of the merchants? How did they raise the capital that they needed? What were the arrangements for obtaining credit? We can only make some logically consistent inferences in answering these questions.

Unlike the commodity merchants, the rich merchants dealt in many commodities. They did not enter into retail trade and functioned as wholesale agents for imported and exported goods. Since they are mentioned as active in overland trade, it would be safe to assume that they organized themselves in groups and carried on overland trade in caravans. For instance, it has been conjectured that the name of Kovalan's father, Masattuvan was derived from his function as *maha-sarthavaha* or the leader of caravans.[74] Furthermore, merchant guilds were well known in ancient India. Two inscriptions dating from the second century BCE from Mangulam in north Madurai and a pottery inscription from Kodumanal in Erode district also referred to *nigamam* or merchant guilds. The *nigamattar*, members of the guild, acting jointly, had carved the stone beds in a cave in Mangulam.[75] The geographical distribution of the inscriptions confirms that the practice of merchants organizing themselves in guilds was widespread.

What were the advantages of the guild as an organization? Being a part of a group lessened risk in two ways. One, it minimized the physical danger of long-distance travel, which was of grave concern while travelling through unsettled and unprotected tracts of the country. It also addressed the disadvantage of trading as an individual merchant, especially in markets in distant lands. The group could also be a possible source of credit for individual members to tide over any short-term needs. Finally, a group identity engendered greater trust in all societies, and members belonging to a guild were perceived to be less risk-prone than individual merchants.

More numerous were the commodity merchants. Contemporary inscriptions refer to merchants dealing in seven different commodities—*aruvai*, cloth; *pon*, gold; *kula*, grains; *uppu*, salt; *ennai*, oil; *kolu*, ploughs; and *panitam*, jaggery.[76] Literary sources also refer to these merchants who mostly conducted their business from their shops in the cities. City streets were segregated according to designated commodities like textiles, gold or grain and such segregation was a characteristic of urban centres all over India till very recent times.

In general, merchants were distinct from artisans or craftsmen who produced or manufactured goods for consumption. Trading was therefore in itself a specialized function requiring specific skills and knowledge. *Silappadikaram* gives a detailed description of the market area of Madurai where each street was devoted to a single product. In the street where gems were sold:

> Flawless diamonds with all the five major attributes as decreed in the ancient texts glowed like the rainbow in white, red, green and dark colours; similarly, there were flawless emeralds; four varieties of perfect rubies; *pushparaga*; honey coloured carnelians which looked like the rays of the sun; sapphires as dark as the night; *gometakam* in red and yellow . . .

Round pearls white and red like Mars which
were free from flaws due to air, sand, stone or water;
corals which were not flawed with holes or bent
because of being caught in rocks under water. In the
street where these nine varieties of gems were sold,
the merchants were highly skilled in assessing the
value and quality of these gemstones; because of
their perfection, this street would never be destroyed
by enemies.[77]

Similarly, in the street of the gold merchants, four
varieties of gold were sold and the merchants were
experts in identifying each variety. Flags were planted as
markers to guide buyers so that they would not get
confused as to where each variety was being sold.[78] In
the street where textiles were sold, hundreds of scented
saris woven intricately with silk and cotton yarn and
wool (rat's hair) were stacked according to variety and
quality in the shops.[79] It is clear that these merchants
were not the artisans who produced the final goods for
the market. Gemstone cutters and jewellers, goldsmiths
and weavers were craftsmen with their own special
skills. The merchants were specialized traders who were
knowledgeable and skilled in assessing the quality and
varieties of the commodities that they handled.

The use of flags to identify shops and the goods sold
was a common business strategy which served to

advertise to the buyers where specific goods would be available. This was particularly true of toddy shops which were found in large numbers in all the cities. In fact, it was noted that the flags marking toddy shops in Puhar were so numerous that sunlight could not penetrate their dense shade.[80]

The *umanar*, salt merchants, were itinerant merchants as opposed to the other commodity merchants who sold their goods in city markets. Sangam poems have wonderfully evocative passages which described the travelling salt merchants. The carts of the salt merchants were drawn by strong bullocks wearing garlands made of pith. Monkeys went along in formation with the carts and played with the children of the salt merchants who were travelling with their parents.[81]

The carts were covered with mats of palmyra leaves, and [each] carried a hen coop on top of the thatch. A small grinding stone and a jar of pickle were slung on the side of the cart which was driven by the wife of the salt merchant who cradled her child in her arms. The merchants had broad, beautiful muscular shoulders. Bullocks were yoked to the crossbar with strong ropes. The merchants went along the carts, guarded them and saw to it that they went in formation . . . They travelled with their many bullocks on a long road which went to many towns.[82]

It is instructive to reconstruct the economics of the trade in salt. To begin with, the salt merchants, unlike the other commodity merchants, were also involved in salt manufacture.[83] Since salt was a low-priced basic necessity of mass consumption, it would not lead to any great value addition through differentiated processes of production and distribution. Salt was essentially location specific in that it was produced only in the coastal areas. The Sangam poems invariably mentioned that ships which had come into the ports with various commodities would exchange them for 'white salt'. However, since salt was consumed universally, it had to be transported overland to all the interior areas. These journeys must have taken many months, which was why the salt merchants travelled with their families, and their carts were virtually their mobile homes. This practice also helped internalize the transport costs for the merchants.

Salt is an essential ingredient for cooking, though it is only consumed in small quantities, as the poets also pointed out. Since it was not a high-priced commodity, the merchants would have operated with only a small profit margin on the base price. Their returns therefore could come only from bulk sales and travelling with their carts enabled them to carry salt in large quantities. On the demand side, a regular supply of salt at specified intervals was not assured throughout the countryside since the inland settlements were totally dependent on the itinerant merchants for their requirements. They would therefore have had to buy salt in large quantities to see them through relatively long periods.

Pepper was the only other commodity mentioned in long-distance overland trade; it was brought from the west in baskets shaped like jackfruit, on pack donkeys.[84] Yet, a great many commodities must have been transported overland, from the ports to the hinterland, to distribute the goods brought in on ships in coastal and long-distance maritime trade, and in the reverse direction, carrying goods from the interior to the ports to be exported. This, in fact, is mentioned in many of the poems.

Overland travel involved danger because of attacks by highway robbers. Though the king Ilantiraiyan was eulogized for maintaining the safety of roads in his kingdom by deploying soldiers armed with bows along forest paths to deter highway robbers, the same poet more realistically also described the bravery of the merchants who armed themselves to fight off highwaymen.[85] Travelling in groups or caravans and being well armed to repel attacks were the strategies adopted to manage the risks of long-distance overland trade.

Urban marketplaces bustled with brisk activity

throughout the day and in the evening. Many craftsmen and artisans produced goods ranging from jewellery and gold to brass- and copper-ware, leather work and ornamental artefacts made of pith, which they sold directly to buyers from their shops. At the lower end of the price scale were people who made and sold food items to the townsfolk and peddlers who sold scented pastes and cosmetics.

Strangely, brokers or intermediaries are rarely mentioned though their services would have been indispensable in markets characterized by highly imperfect information, especially in view of the large number of foreign traders who came to trade in the region. The *Silappadikaram* refers to people who rendered 'small services'[86] who might have been offering brokerage services. In Madurai, brokers roamed day and night along the street of the grain market, with weighing scales and measures.[87]

## Foreign traders and merchant diaspora

Because of the voluminous trade carried on with Rome, foreign merchants were very visible in the port cities. Though in general the term yavana was supposed to refer to the Romans, in reality, the yavana were probably traders and sailors of many nationalities from the eastern Mediterranean region. In Puhar:

In the harbour area was the quarters of the yavana whose eye-catching goods were in great demand. Foreign traders who had left their native places and come here to make money, sailing their ships across dark seas, lived in residential quarters close to the sea, as if they were all of one nationality.[88]

It was noted that 'on the beachfront lived the merchants who had come overseas to trade'.[89] These merchants traded on their own account, and their goods were stamped with their name, weight and measure and kept in the official warehouse.[90] In the coastal areas of the Pandya kingdom, 'people who sail their ships across the oceans come together and sell their horses in exchange for goods brought by the coastal ships'.[91] But foreign traders also travelled inland, and were often seen in Madurai, the largest city in Tamilakam. That cities were multicultural centres where many languages were heard was evidently a source of pride, and the fact was repeated several times by the Sangam poets. However, the Tamils as the host society displayed an ambivalent attitude towards the foreign merchants who needed to stay for extended periods in Tamilakam. In Puhar, for instance, while the foreign merchants were allowed to trade freely, they had to live in a separate settlement which segregated them from the local residents. There are several references in Sangam poems to yavana, but it can be seen that the attitude towards the yavana was often hostile, and that they were considered an alien, even barbaric, people who spoke a harsh-sounding language.[92] This instinctive suspicion of the foreigner persisted even though many yavana and other foreigners who came from across the seas had stayed on in the Tamil region and worked in various capacities, often as skilled craftsmen. The fortress gate of the city of Madurai was guarded by yavana carrying large swords,[93] while the inner apartment of the king was guarded by deaf-mute *mlecchas*, barbarians.[94] There are references to yavana metal workers as 'hard-eyed yavana' (perhaps because they had grey or blue eyes) who fashioned tiger chains with strong links and lamps,[95] and of yavana carpenters who worked on the royal pavilion in Puhar.[96] Trade thus paved the way for migration and cross-cultural interchange.

There are almost no references in the literary sources to Tamil merchant diaspora in overseas settlements. Sri Lanka (Ilam) and Java (Savakam) were frequented by the Tamil people, and Buddhism was the overarching unifying factor which brought together the three countries. Gajabahu, the king of Sri Lanka, came to worship at the temple dedicated to Kannagi built by the Chera king Chenguttuvan.[97] Java, in particular, is mentioned almost as if it were an extension of

Tamilakam, indicating steady commercial and cultural intercourse. However there is some evidence that the Tamil people did travel and live in other parts of South-East Asia. A stone with a Tamil Brahmi inscription dating to the third or fourth century CE has been discovered in Thailand. The inscription referred to a goldsmith and the stone has been identified as the touchstone of a goldsmith,[98] suggesting that people from Tamilakam travelled to centres in South-East Asia to live and trade there.

## URBANIZATION

Urbanization was a natural concomitant of trade, of an economy which had diversified beyond subsistence into producing for a market. The process of urbanization was built on several prerequisites which included a well-developed agricultural sector, a diversified economy, physical structures like buildings and monuments and a complex social structure.[99] What are the sources which will help to reconstruct the urban landscape and the process of urbanization? Many ports and inland towns found mention in contemporary foreign accounts (Ptolemy, *Periplus*) and have also been identified in archaeological excavations. However, we need to go to the descriptions in literary works not only to understand the urban topography and how cities functioned, but also to relive the essence of urban living in ancient times.

The major inland cities mentioned in the Sangam poems, that is, the four capital cities of Madurai, Karur (Vanji), Uraiyur and Kanchi, continue to exist even today, though the ruins of the ancient city of Madurai are located to the south of the present city, and Uraiyur is now a suburb of Tiruchi, across the river Kaveri. Most of the ports, however, have dwindled to coastal villages though the settlements can be identified. This might have happened due to two factors. First, the Coromandel Coast historically did not have any natural harbours. Coastal settlements grew to be important ports for various external reasons, mostly political, and faded into obscurity once the political situation changed. Second, there have been changes to the coastline because of natural phenomena like the sea receding in some parts or giant tidal waves causing destruction. The total eclipse of Puhar as a major trade emporium and as a port is a case in point.

The cities of the ancient period were probably not very large, though some were described as managaram or the great city. For instance, in *Silappadikaram*, an angry Kannagi seeking to avenge the death of Kovalan 'went around Madurai thrice', suggesting that the city covered a relatively small area. But in the final analysis, there was a clear perception that the city represented a pattern of settlement which was distinct and different from rural habitats.

Cities were characterized by a concentration of population and economic activities. All cities, including ports, were protected by defensive fortress walls which were so constructed that vats of boiling oil could be poured on attacking armies and archers could shoot them without being targeted themselves. In all the cities, houses are invariably described as tall structures 'reaching to the sky', with windows to let in the breeze and terraces where residents could enjoy moonlit nights. However stylized this description might be it probably represented the reality of houses huddled in a relatively restricted space. Such tall buildings with windows are depicted in sculptures in ancient historical sites like Sanchi.

The hustle and bustle of cities is best captured in the descriptions of Puhar, the premier port, and Madurai, the great capital. Many features were common to both cities: the organization of urban space, segregation of residential and commercial areas, as well as separate areas or streets assigned for various occupations and traders, and the visible presence of foreigners speaking many languages, all of which are described many times.

Statue of the Buddha
recovered from the sea

Wharf in Puhar

Figure 2.2 Poompuhar Excavations
(Courtesy: Tamil Nadu State Department
of Archaeology)

# Puhar

Puhar was divided into two main areas, Maruvurpakkam
along the sea and Pattinappakkam which was further
inland. Maruvurpakkam, where the foreign merchants
including the yavana had their quarters, was primarily
the commercial area. Here peddling traders roamed the
streets selling coloured and aromatic pastes and incense;
weavers had their own quarters; broad streets were piled
so high with silk, coral, sandalwood, eaglewood, flawless
pearls, precious gems and gold that they could not be
measured; heaps of grain and many other goods lined

the streets; areas were segregated for people selling sweets, fish, toddy, white salt, meat and oil. There was also a separate area where artisans like brass- and copper-smiths, jewellers, tailors, leather workers and others lived.[100] In Pattinappakkam lived the rich Perunkudi merchants, as well as Brahmins who recited the Vedas, farmers, doctors and astrologers. Though some artisans such as pearl jewellers and conch cutters also lived in this district, the residents were primarily engaged in various service activities like bards, dancers, courtesans and prostitutes. Soldiers and men who rode horses and elephants lived outside the fort,[101] and were presumably intended to defend the port.

The market street was between these two districts where the voices of the buyers and sellers of goods were heard continuously.[102] Perhaps the ambience and energy of Puhar are best captured in the description of the harbour area at night:

> Traders had lit lamps in their shops selling coloured pastes, flowers, cosmetic powders and eatables. The lights in the places of the skilled goldsmiths who made jewellery; the rows of lights kept by merchants selling sweet dishes; lamps on top of pots put up by merchants who sold other eatables; lamps lit by women selling toddy; the lights of the fish sellers; the lighthouse which guided ships at sea; the lamps

kept by fishermen in their boats; by people from various countries; by the guards of the warehouse, Puhar was lit up with all these lights.[103]

Puhar was administered by five groups of state officials and eight corporate assemblies.[104] This administrative framework probably functioned throughout the region including rural settlements, and the village assembly was referred to in an ancient inscription.[105] According to the *Manimekalai* Puhar was virtually destroyed by a tidal wave with much loss of life, an occurrence described as *kadal kol* or taken by the sea. The theme of loss occasioned by the sea is a recurrent one in historical memory in Tamil culture, and the loss of a significant volume of early literary works in Tamil is usually attributed to a major incursion by the sea. We can only close with a hypothesis: was this the reason for the decline of Puhar as a port?

## Madurai

Madurai was universally accepted as the oldest city in Tamilakam. Also referred to as Kudal, it was famous for its towers and was known as *nanmadakkudal*, the city of four towers; *kodimadakkudal*, the city of towers with flags; and as the city with beautiful chariots.[106] Madurai was encircled by a fearsome fortress wall surrounded by a moat and a strong hedge. There was an underground passage beneath the moat which was wide enough for an elephant to cross to reach the fort gate. Guarded by yavana carrying large swords, Madurai looked as grand as the opened jewellery casket of Indra himself.[107] Madurai was so large and populous that, 'like the ocean, which does not overflow or dry up, Madurai with its towers did not diminish when people took goods away nor did it become overcrowded when more and more people came in . . . Madurai is as immeasurable as the Ganga flowing into the sea, with ships bringing tribute and many goods each day.'[108]

Poets noted that the high level of activity in the cities was reflected in a high volume of noise.

> In the street of the day market, the sounds in the evening were as loud as when a festival was being celebrated in Madurai with its towers . . . Merchants from foreign countries unload the goods they have brought by ship to exchange [them] for gems and jewellery. These sounds mingle with the sounds from the city, and the noise from the evening shops resembles the chatter of birds returning to their nests.[109]

Courtesans were an important part of urban society. Silappadikaram has lengthy descriptions of courtesans, their accomplishments and their lifestyles in Puhar and

Madurai. According to the sociocultural values of ancient Tamilakam, courtesans were not looked down upon as social outcasts; on the contrary, they were esteemed members of society who added to the quality of life in urban areas. Though they were described as women who did not have husbands or cohabit with only one partner, they were seen as being different and much superior to prostitutes 'who sold themselves each day'.

There were many temples in Puhar and Madurai. There were temples to major Hindu deities like Siva, Vishnu, Murugan and Balarama. Several traditional, indigenous deities and supernatural spirits were also venerated and worshipped. Besides these, Buddhism and Jainism were important religions in Tamilakam. Madurai, for instance, had temples dedicated to Mahavira and Buddha.[110] In fact, these two religions were central to the two major Tamil epics *Silappadikaram* and *Manimekalai.*

*

What were the factors behind urbanization? It is important to understand that the level of urban development should not be overstated, in spite of the literary references to the vigour and vitality of cities. In fact, only two types of urban settlements are mentioned in Sangam literature—capital cities in the interior and ports on the coast. The description in *Silappadikaram* of the route taken by Kovalan and Kannagi from Puhar to Madurai in search of a new start in their life mentions only one city—Uraiyur, the Chola capital. Otherwise, the couple went through fertile agricultural land crossing many waterways and villages. Tamilakam was predominantly rural with limited urbanization. Commerce was the driving force behind the development of ports, while capital cities were the seats of political authority.[111]

But one must be careful also not to underestimate the economic dynamics of urbanization in Tamilakam. Ancient Tamilakam had achieved a high level of economic activity given the technological constraints of the time. Trade had evolved as a specialized activity, distinct from production. The extent of maritime trade and contact with overseas markets from Rome to China was reflected in a high level of mercantile activity. While it is true that cities were not numerous, they nevertheless contributed significantly to the development of a variety of manufactures and skilled crafts. The urban environment in which merchants of many nations were free to live and trade without hindrance and where many religions coexisted and flourished reflected the positive attitude of the Tamil kings towards trade and business.

# 3. STATE, POLITY AND OVERSEAS RELATIONS UNDER THE TAMIL KINGDOMS

WE RETURN TO the Tamil region after a gap of three centuries following the period of the Sangam literature, a dark and amorphous period shrouded in mystery for which no information is available to reconstruct the history of the region.[1] These missing centuries are generally referred to as the 'Kalabhra interregnum' when Tamilakam came under the control of a non-Tamil race, the Kalabhras. Nothing much is known about them though they were described as an 'evil force' in Tamil works, and they were eventually overthrown in the sixth century CE by the Pallavas in northern Tamilakam and by the Pandya king in the south.

The absence of historical records does not mean a static period marked by absence of change or a period of cultural decline. During these centuries Jainism and Buddhism made major inroads into Tamilakam and became dominant religions supported by the rulers, and from these religions came the authors of the major Tamil epics. Nor is there any reason to believe that trade or economic activity, in general, were disrupted to any degree during this period. What we lack is the continuity that historical data would provide for understanding the transition from the ancient to the early medieval period.

## POLITICAL CONSOLIDATION UNDER TAMIL EMPIRES

Two major empires emerged in the Tamil region after the overthrow of Kalabhra rule in the sixth century, namely the Pallavas in the north who ruled from Kanchipuram and the Pandyas in the south who ruled from Madurai, their traditional capital. The Cholas at this time were completely marginalized, till they rose as a major power in the tenth century.

The reign of the 'great Pallavas' began with Simhavishnu in the mid sixth century. Simhavishnu is credited with many victories, including an invasion of Sri Lanka. This was the first of several naval expeditions to Sri Lanka by Tamil rulers which had many long-ranging political and economic implications since commerce usually followed conquest. Most importantly, this expedition indicated the presence of a navy capable of moving troops and even elephants across seas.[2] Pallava coins with the emblem of ships with two masts indicate the importance of shipping in the affairs of the kingdom.

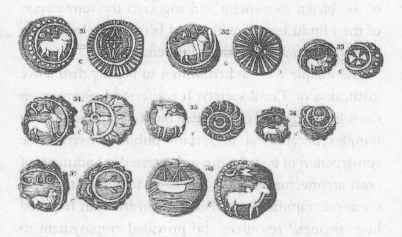

Figure 3.1 Emblems on Pallava Coins: Lithographic Reproduction
(Source: Walter Elliot, *Coins of South India*)

The event which had the most significant long-term impact on Tamil society and polity was arguably the revival of Hinduism during the reign of the early Pallavas, popularly ascribed to the reign of Mahendravarman I (590 CE to 629 CE). Though not supported by hard historical evidence, according to the hagiographic account of the Saivite saints of Tamilakam, the revival of Hinduism began when the saint Tirunavukkarasar reconverted from Jainism to Saivism. The Pallava king too followed soon after. Some decades later, the Pandyan king was reconverted from Jainism by Jnanasambandar, another Saivite saint. This revival marked the beginning of the bhakti movement and triggered the reinvention of the Hindu temple which had been in decline at the height of Jain and Buddhist influence.

The temple was, and continues to be, the distinctive institution of Tamil society. It conferred legitimacy on the ruling and social elite, so that building and supporting temples became an important public activity. The construction of temples not only created monuments of great architectural beauty; it was an activity with many economic ramifications. Temple construction required huge financial resources and provided employment to many artisans and craftsmen. Temples were also major economic entities in their own right, as employers, landowners and consumers of a variety of goods and services, including imported luxuries.

Temples were the central institutions around which local administrative institutions revolved, so that all transactions relating to local resource management were recorded in temple inscriptions. Besides this, temples

were the nodes which triggered the growth of urban
centres, a process that was intrinsic to the growth of
commerce. In the eighth century, the robber chief turned
Vaishnavite saint or *alvar* of the bhakti movement
Tirumangai Alvar, who was a contemporary of
Nandivarman II, a later Pallava king, described the
development of a town around the temple in
Tiruvallikkeni, modern Triplicane in the heart of
Chennai. He wrote, 'Tiruvallikkeni has towers and
groves with honeybees; it has been laid out by the
Tondaiman, "Pallava king", with wells, outer walls,
towering monuments and many structures.'[3] Similarly,
Kanchipuram, the capital, which saw an explosion of
temple construction during the Pallava period, was
described as 'beautiful Kanchi, surrounded by ponds
and a fortress wall, with magnificent tall towers and
mansions'.[4]

Pallava rule also saw the development of
Mamallapuram as the major port of the Coromandel
Coast which was frequented by 'boats carrying treasure
which captivated the senses, elephants and loads of
precious gems'.[5] Mamallapuram continued to be the
main port until it was superseded by Nagapattinam
under the Cholas. By the early eighth century, the
eminence of the Pallava king Rajasimha
Narasimhavarman II had spread far and emissaries were

being exchanged with the court of the Chinese emperor. Narasimhavarman II was referred to as Sha-li-Na-lo-seng-k'ia-pa-to-pa-ma, Sri Narasimha Potavarman, in the Chinese chronicles. The exchanges included a proposal from the Pallava king in 720 to use his war elephants and cavalry to fight the Arabs and Tibetans, and a request from the Chinese emperor that Narasimhavarman should build a Buddhist temple in his kingdom for the use of Chinese visitors.[6]

One of the last of the great Pallavas was Nandivarman II whose long rule lasted for sixty-five years. Interestingly, he was elected king by the officials of the capital, the college of learned Brahmins and the people when he was barely twelve years old in 731, when the direct line of the Pallavas had died out throwing the kingdom into turmoil. He was said to be a prince of the collateral branch of the family which had been ruling in Champa in what is now Vietnam.[7] Details of his coronation are carved in bas-reliefs on the outer wall of the Vaikuntha Perumal temple of Kanchipuram. The main points of interest here are the indication of the close links between the Tamil kingdoms and the Hindu kingdoms of South-East Asia, as also the strength of the local polity who stepped in to choose a ruler to end the political crisis in the kingdom.

The four centuries of Pallava rule embodied the many

features which characterized Tamil polity and commercial activity during the early medieval period. These included strong local institutions, the rise of temples which were pivotal in energizing the interaction of local administrative bodies with merchant organizations, and extended relations with the kingdoms of South-East Asia both through military intervention and through commercial and cultural interchange.

The Pallava kingdom faded away during the tenth century giving way to the Chola dynasty which dominated the Tamil region from the mid-tenth century till the late twelfth century before finally disintegrating in the latter part of the thirteenth century. During this period the Cholas came out of the shadow of subordination to the Pallavas and Pandyas, and, by the beginning of the eleventh century, they ruled over all of south India. The western part of south India under the Cheras had by this time acquired a distinct Kerala identity, while the south-eastern part of peninsular India, now known as Tamilakam, was under the rule of the Cholas and the Pallavas. The southern part commonly known as Cholamandalam or the Coromandel was controlled by the Cholas, while the northern area known as Tondaimandalam was ruled by the Pallavas. The first great emperor of the Cholas was Rajaraja I who came to the throne towards the end of the tenth century. Under him the Chola state grew to become an empire when he defeated the Pandya and Kerala kings. Parts of Mysore were also incorporated into the kingdom. He also invaded northern Sri Lanka, continuing the tradition of military and political intervention in the island kingdom, and this resulted in a substantial presence of Tamil merchant groups in Sri Lanka.

The Chola empire scaled even greater heights under his son Rajendra I. His military campaigns extended north up to the river Ganga, which earned him the title of Gangaikondacholan. He sent a naval expedition against the Sailendra empire to the Malay Peninsula. When Kulottunga I, the grandson of Rajendra I (r. 1070 to 1122), became the Chola emperor, the kingdom of the eastern Chalukyas was incorporated into the Chola empire, extending the territory up to north coastal Andhra.

Political consolidation under the Cholas was accompanied by administrative reforms. New revenue divisions were created for more efficient tax collection, as will be described in the section on local administration. Chola administration was driven primarily by the concerns of raising revenue in their own territory and managing local administrative bodies. But the kings also followed an aggressive policy of conquest and territorial expansion, fuelled by imperial ambitions as well as to add to the territory and revenue resources of the empire. The Chola emperors were also aware of the need to promote and protect the commercial interests of Tamil merchant groups, especially in their overseas trade in the Indian Ocean region. This consideration dominated their relations with countries further east, especially the kingdom of Sri Vijaya (modern Palembang) in Sumatra and China, as well as Sri Lanka, their immediate neighbour. Their interactions fluctuated between diplomatic and cordial relationships to military intervention, as will be seen in the next section.

## LOCAL ADMINISTRATION AND CORPORATE ASSEMBLIES

The Tamil region had a distinctive and highly complex administrative structure which had evolved even before political consolidation under successive Tamil kingdoms. The economy of the region was primarily agrarian and the management of the two major natural resources, land and water, was the primary concern for the economy and society. A related issue was the collection of revenue from agriculture. A hierarchy of local administrative bodies was in place for resource management and revenue collection.

## Local assemblies[8]

The hierarchy of administrative units began with the village or *ur* as the smallest unit, followed by the *nadu* or sub-region, while the *kottam*, district or region, was the largest unit. The affairs of the village and the nadu were handled by local assemblies. This system of local autonomy and decentralized administration predated the advent of the Pallava and early Pandya kingdoms in the sixth century and resulted in the optimum utilization of resources and most efficient governance in the absence of powerful kings or centralized states.

A further category of village was created under Pallava rule with the establishment of Brahmin villages known as *brahmadeya* through land grants to Brahmins. These villages also had their own assembly. The creation of this new category of village was probably motivated by several objectives. At the functional level, this resulted in the extension of agriculture by bringing more land under cultivation leading to a rise in land prices because of the increased transactions in land. This consequently increased the cash flow in different localities. At the ideological level, the grants of land to Brahmins also lent greater legitimacy to the kings because of the social value placed on Brahmins and Brahminical ideology. Several historians have also pointed out that the creation of the brahmadeya village served an additional political purpose. These villages were first established under the Pallavas when they were creating a powerful empire in Tamilakam, the pace of development increasing under the Cholas who had the largest empire in Tamil history. Thus, the creation of a new category of villages which owed its existence to the king served to dilute the autonomy and authority of the older nadu and ur assemblies, which was of advantage to the growing power of the kings. With this intervention, the ur became the non-Brahmin village, while the brahmadeya was inhabited primarily by Brahmins.

The fourth administrative unit was the urban marketing centre or *nagaram*, which also had its own assembly. Though the nagarams were essentially concerned with managing local trade and merchants, they also had jurisdiction over agricultural lands in the neighbourhood of towns, indicating that the distinction between urban and rural was quite nebulous during the medieval period. There were very few nagarams during Pallava rule but they increased in number under the Cholas which definitely reflected a process of urban and commercial growth. Thus, nagarams were the markers of increased trade and mercantile activity, and their functioning will be discussed in greater detail in the next chapter.

The local assemblies of each administrative unit were

known by the same name as the geographical unit, ur, nadu and nagaram. The assembly of the brahmadeya village was known as the *sabha*. The members of the assemblies were known as the *urar, nattar, sabhaiyar* and *nagarattar*,[9] people of the ur, nadu, sabha and nagaram. Generally all adult males were members of the assembly, so that decisions taken by the assemblies were deemed to have the sanction of the entire village or town. The sabha however had a more complex structure, with selected administrative committees known as *variyam* which were specifically in charge of managing the temple or water and land resources of the village. In addition, sabhas had a ruling committee known as *alunganattar.* Nagarams also had their own committees or variyams. The management of the finances and functioning of local temples was a primary responsibility of the assemblies, and often all three, the ur, sabha and nagaram, were jointly in charge of the affairs of the local temple.

An obvious query that comes to mind is: why did a state rapidly growing in territory and power encourage autonomous, decentralized centres of power to continue and even grow? There could be many reasons for this. Primarily, it was not politically expedient for the rulers to abolish local institutions. Local assemblies, mentioned even in the *Silappadikaram*, had evolved at a time when the conditions were conducive for their growth because political authority in the Tamil region was fragmented and lacked stability. By creating a democratic structure which involved the participation of all local inhabitants and the acceptance that all decisions were consensual, the assemblies were more egalitarian in their functioning than perhaps any other form of administration. The local people therefore had a significant stake in maintaining their autonomy and independence in making decisions and the abolition of these institutions could be possible only at great political cost and loss of legitimacy for the kings. While interventions did occur, mainly through the establishment of brahmadeya villages, there was no overt interference in the functioning or affairs of the ur, nadu, nagaram or sabha.

From a practical point of view, the local assemblies represented the most efficient form of organization under the existing conditions of communications and technology. An empire, fast expanding territorially, could never have imposed centralized administration effectively across the entire kingdom. Thus, while the central authority levied taxes and played a supervisory role, tax collection was left to the local bodies as the most cost-effective option. These corporate assemblies also exercised judicial powers. Two inscriptions dating to the early eleventh century can be cited here. A merchant of Jambai in South Arcot district[10] had to deposit a fine in gold with the local ur in the memory of a man he had killed while the latter was trying to assault the merchant's wife. In another case, occurring in the same town, a local official had to pay a fine as atonement for the suicide of a woman whom he had hounded for taxes, the fine being deposited with the nagaram.[11]

At the village level, checks on the power of the state were also an important consideration. If one could use the terminology from institutional economics, the local assemblies with their autonomy involved the least transaction costs to all levels of government and society at large. The state did not have to incur the cost of maintaining an expensive and elaborate bureaucracy which would not have functioned efficiently given the constraints of the existing conditions of communication. Local bodies knew their constituents and local conditions and could act in a manner acceptable to the people; they were therefore the optimal institutions of administration. The local assemblies, in fact, survived various empires, including that of the Cholas, which is a testimony to their continued relevance in the medieval period.

## Revenue administration and taxation[12]

The authority of the state to collect taxes was clearly accepted, and revenue administration constituted an important part of state policy and functioning. The Chola state played a proactive role in reforming revenue administration by creating new revenue divisions called the *mandalam* and new revenue districts known as *valanadu* replacing earlier revenue regions. The mandalam was the largest unit in revenue management with an officer in charge of maintaining the register of the revenue collected and of administration. Functionally, it was the intermediary level between the central treasury and local bodies which resulted in greater accountability and control in revenue collection. Matters relating to the revenue of the nadu were decided by the local assembly, the nattar. The village was the basic unit in charge of revenue collection and the village assemblies—the ur, sabha and nagaram—were responsible for the collection of taxes.

Taxation under the Cholas was also an amalgam of the existing and the new. Several new revenue terms were introduced and superimposed on pre-existing traditional terms. In the main, there were only two groups of taxes levied on the two foremost economic activities, agriculture and commerce. It is difficult to determine the degree of monetization of the economy and tax administration. However, it can be deduced from inscriptions that land taxes were paid in paddy, while commercial taxes were usually paid in money.

Since land was the most important productive resource in the predominantly agrarian economy of medieval India, land tax was naturally the most important source of revenue. The issue of land revenue needs to be discussed with respect to two parameters, land ownership and tax rates. There is little doubt that the Chola state did not own land. Private ownership with rights of alienation and inheritance rights with regard to land were clearly recognized. But the local assemblies, the ur and sabha, also owned and could dispose of land which was commonly owned. By and large, private ownership was more common in the brahmadeyas and communal ownership vested in the ur, though as the Chola state weakened, the incidence of private ownership increased in the urs also.[13]

According to the *dharmasastras*, the tax rate had to be fixed at one-sixth of the value of the produce. The actual tax rates, however, were much higher and sometimes went up to as much as 40 per cent. It must be remembered that many taxes were also collected by the local bodies for their own revenue, which had to be added to the taxes paid to the state. In general, the tax rate was probably around one-third of the gross produce.[14] Land revenue, however, could not be levied at a fixed rate without taking the productivity of land into account. Therefore, a highly sophisticated system of assessment was followed based on land surveys which were undertaken periodically to assess the productivity of land in order to fix the tax levels.[15] Thus, revenue assessment was higher on wet or irrigated land than on dry or unirrigated land, while tax was levied on a graduated scale on land recently brought into cultivation. The land tax was, in fact, a bundle of taxes levied on land, cultivators and other forms of cess, including a water tax on lands which used water from a common source of irrigation. Local assemblies also levied cess for the maintenance and desilting of local tanks or lakes. Compulsory levy of labour and provision of cooked food for state officials visiting a locality on duty were also a part of the land tax.

Taxation was generally kept at a politically feasible level. This might not have been due to any exaggerated sense of *rajadharma*, just governance, since practical considerations had to be taken into account; otherwise, oppressively high taxes would prove to be counter-productive. Many individual instances of misbehaviour by tax collecting officials and extortion were reported,[16] but these were sporadic rather than systemic when the Chola state was functioning effectively. Excessive taxation and oppression were more characteristic of the failed state and occurred when kingdoms were disintegrating and central authority had weakened. These episodes were commonly reported after the thirteenth century and triggered popular protest on a mass scale, when local inhabitants took to leaving a habitation and moving to new locations.

Taxes on commercial activities and on professions constituted the second major source of revenue, and are of special interest in a study on trade and commerce. These were quite comprehensive and were levied on virtually every aspect of economic activity outside agriculture. *Sungam*, tolls, were collected on goods in transit on highways. Taxes were levied on shops and goods traded, either by weight or by volume. Merchants had to pay taxes as individuals, and these were levied on *chetti*s, local merchants, and on *sonaka*s, foreign merchants, mostly Arab. This classification itself is of interest since it shows that foreign merchants were living and trading within the Tamil region as residents. All the other professions were also taxed, important among them being goldsmiths, weavers, oil mongers, blacksmiths and potters. Even shepherds, washermen and fishermen fell within the ambit of taxation. Implements used in production, like the blacksmith's furnace, the weaver's loom and oil presses, were also taxed.

The range of taxes which were levied is indicative of the extent to which the state at the central and local levels intervened in all economic activities. This becomes evident from the list of taxes collected by the ur and the nagaram. An eleventh-century inscription notes that several taxes collected by the ur were assigned to be used for special pujas for the birthday of the king. These included taxes of the ur, tax to be paid to the temple; tax on fishing; on using the river; on goldsmiths; several small taxes; tax on woven cloth; the 10 per cent of collected taxes which was assigned for public works; taxes on lands; taxes to pay soldiers; on right- and left-hand castes;[17] monthly tax; contributory labour and ten *kasus* which had to be paid for each man.[18] Even after the Chola period the range of taxes did not change to any extent, so that the administrative system of the Cholas remained stable for more than two centuries. A thirteenth-century inscription again refers to the taxes which were assigned to a local temple. These included taxes on irrigated and unirrigated land paid in paddy; taxes on gold and other taxes paid in cash; taxes paid on looms; by goldsmiths; taxes paid to maintain the accountant of the ur; taxes paid by individuals and by the merchants; taxes on oil presses; taxes on the use of common cattle sheds and ponds; taxes collected by the nadu and by the ur.[19] Taxes collected by the nagaram were equally extensive. The articles taxed included flowers in shops, lime trees, dry crops, red water-lilies, areca nut, betel leaves, saffron, ginger and sugar cane, as well as taxes collected from the merchants and different professional artisans.[20]

The land taxes and commercial taxes were remitted to the central treasury. Officials to supervise and audit the collection of taxes were posted in the hierarchy of administrative divisions above the village. However, levies of labour and other local cess would have been in the domain of the village. The central government also assigned taxes to different local assemblies and temples, which allowed for a system of revenue sharing. Local bodies also had the authority to grant exemption from taxes, especially to temples.

Supervision and auditing of revenue collection were important functions which were undertaken with diligence. It is clear that on matters relating to tax collection the state bureaucracy interacted only with the corporate assemblies which were held accountable for any lapses in revenue mobilization. This system continued to be in force well into the thirteenth century, even when the Chola Empire was beginning to disintegrate, and all corporate assemblies—nagaram, sabha and ur—were routinely under the scanner with regard to tax collection.

The principle of collective, corporate responsibility was clearly in force, and in 1266, when individual owners could not pay taxes even after borrowing money from various sources, the village assembly was ordered to pay the arrears, for which they had to sell the lands and house sites under the assembly to the temple to raise the required money.[21] In 1003, when the accounts of the nagaram of Tirunavalur, South Arcot district, and other *devadana* villages were checked, it was found that taxes to be paid in paddy and gold had not been remitted. The nagarattar of Tirunavalur had to pay the back taxes in paddy and gold.[22] In 1125, the sabha of Tiruvadi in South Arcot district met to discuss the shortfall in the payment of taxes, and agreed to sell a part of the common land to a merchant.[23] Finally, in 1267–68, the ur of Visalur (modern Kudimiyamalai) in Pudukkottai district had to sell land for 64,000 kasu on the orders of two officers of the king and the nattar. The urar had been in default in the payment of taxes for a long time, and also had to account for 50,000 kasu which had been deposited with them to be used for the renovation of the temple.[24]

Tax collection and revenue administration went through four distinctive stages, which were in tandem with the rise and decline of Chola rule over three centuries. *Puravi vari*, the department of revenue, was first enlarged and consolidated during the tenth century. During the eleventh century, under the strong rule of Rajaraja I and his son Rajendra I, revenue collection was maximized with a corresponding increase in the bureaucracy which was in charge of revenue administration. The great increase in public spending during this period as evidenced in the construction of great temples by the two emperors was an index of the increase in revenue. The central power of the Chola kings began to decline from the time of Kulottunga I, and in the century following the beginning of his reign in 1070, there was a noticeable decline in the size of the bureaucracy, matching the decline in revenue collection. From the last quarter of the twelfth century when Chola power was going into eclipse, revenue collection as well as centralized revenue administration showed a sharp deterioration.[25]

## CULTURAL AND COMMERCIAL CONTACTS: SOUTH-EAST ASIA AND CHINA

Diplomatic and commercial contacts with the kingdoms of South-East Asia dominated the foreign policy of the Tamil kingdoms from the time of the Pallavas. Occasionally, the kingdoms also followed an aggressive route of military intervention which served both strategic political and commercial objectives, albeit with limited success in the short run.

## The Hindu kingdoms

From the middle of the fourth century CE, various kingdoms of South-East Asia extending from Thailand to Vietnam in the east, and the Indonesian islands in the south, were ruled by Hindu kings of Indian origin,[26] so that the region virtually became a 'greater India'.[27] The presence of Indians in the South-East Asian countries was not confined only to rulers; military officials, priests, Brahmins and traders and professional craftsmen had also migrated to these countries, as can be noted from the corpus of inscriptions discovered across the entire region. This overseas expansion did not come about as a result of military conquest. The experience of the naval attacks on the Sailendra empire and even in Sri Lanka, which is much nearer to south India, proved that such victories tended to be of short duration and colonization or control built on military initiatives was not sustainable. The expansion based on commercial and cultural interactions, on the other hand, was long-lasting. The most outstanding visible monuments of this cultural synthesis are to be seen in the magnificent temples of Angkor in Cambodia, built by the great Kambuja king Suryavarman II in the twelfth century. However, there are many other lesser monuments all over South-East Asia which attest to this synthesis.

Initially, Hinduism spread rapidly in all South-East

Asian kingdoms primarily because the kings were Hindus and also because religious teachers from India helped propagate Hinduism under the patronage of the kings. Indigenous social and religious culture was also conducive to the assimilation of Hindu beliefs and values. Gradually Buddhism took root in these kingdoms and has remained the major religion in most countries in South-East Asia from Burma to Vietnam, the only exceptions being Malaysia and Indonesia where Islam is the major religion.

For more than one millennium, these kingdoms retained strong links with India through religious and cultural interactions. However, China was the great empire and political power for the entire region and embassies were regularly sent to the Chinese court by all the kingdoms—Champa, Kambuja and the Sailendras of Sri Vijaya—which implicitly acknowledged the superior status of China as a superpower both politically and economically. The embassies sent to China by the Chola emperors, Rajaraja I in 1015, Rajendra I in 1033 and Kulottunga I in 1077, in effect accepted the centrality of China for maintaining the political and economic power balance in the region.

The nature of Indian influence in South-East Asia can be seen in the inscriptions that have been discovered throughout the region. The preponderant majority of the inscriptions are in Sanskrit and more than thirty inscriptions on stone and many on other artefacts, especially votive offerings on clay tablets or gold leaf, have been discovered in Vietnam, Laos, Malaysia, Indonesia and Thailand.[28] Most refer to religious gifts by local kings; some are eulogies of the local king but have no other context; a few refer to the teachings of Buddha. These inscriptions reflect the characteristics of a pan-Indian influence in terms of the language used— Sanskrit and Sanskritized Prakrit—as well as the religious synthesis of the three major religions of India, and especially Hinduism and Buddhism. The strong Tamil influence, however, is evident in the script used in the inscriptions. With a couple of rare exceptions most are in southern Brahmi of the sixth to seventh century or the Pallava grantha script. The predominant use of the southern Brahmi and Pallava scripts which were on occasion adapted to local phonetics leads to the inference that the South-East Asian societies had assimilated the Tamil scripts over the centuries due to a process of acculturation resulting from the presence of a substantial Tamil population in these kingdoms. It also suggests that in addition to people of Tamil origin employed by the kings and in the courts, many of these migrants must have been merchants trading in these countries.

This inference is further corroborated by the Tamil

inscriptions which are very few in number compared to the more prolific use of Sanskrit as a ceremonial language. Only seven inscriptions in Tamil have been discovered in South-East Asia.[29] The time frame of the inscriptions ranges over one thousand years, from the third or fourth century CE to the thirteenth century, which again supports the inference of long-standing cultural and commercial intercourse between the Tamil country and South-East Asia. The earliest is the inscription on the touchstone of a goldsmith, in Tamil Brahmi script, discovered in Thailand (referred to in chapter 2). The other six inscriptions date from the ninth to the thirteenth century, of which three refer directly to the activities of merchant guilds from Tamilakam. The inscription at Takua Pa in southern Thailand, strategically located in the northern coast of the Malay Peninsula, refers to a tank which was named Sri Avaninaranam and placed under the protection of members of the Manigramam guild as well as some other groups. It must be noted that Avaninaranan was one of the titles of the Pallava king Nandivarman III who ruled in the mid-ninth century. Here, we also see a custom which was common across Tamilakam whereby such public works and places were given the same name as that of the king or of members of the royal family. That the tank was made the responsibility of the

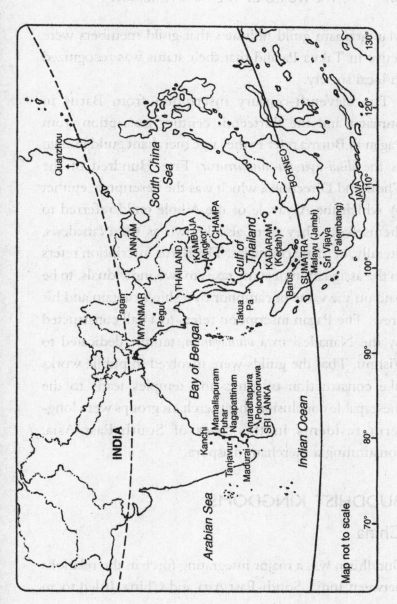

Map 3.1 Tamilakam and South-East Asia

Map not to scale

Manigramam guild indicates that guild members were active in Takua Pa and that their status was recognized in local society.

The eleventh-century inscription from Barus in Sumatra and the thirteenth century inscription from Pagan in Burma refer to the large merchant guild known as the *disai-ayirattu-ainnurruvar*, Five Hundred of the Thousand Directions, which was the descriptive epithet by which the Ayyavole or the Aihole guild referred to themselves. They were also known as the Nanadesis, literally, of many countries. The Barus inscription refers to the assignation of some taxes to two individuals, to be paid on the value of camphor by a ship's captain and his crew. The Pagan inscription refers to a hall constructed by the Nanadesi in a *vinnagaram*, temple dedicated to Vishnu. That the guilds were involved in public works like construction of tanks and temples leads to the inescapable conclusion that merchant groups were long-term residents in the cities of South-East Asia, constituting a merchant diaspora.

# BUDDHIST KINGDOMS
## China

Buddhism was a major integrating force in the relations between India, South-East Asia and China. It led to an increase in travel between these countries by Buddhist pilgrims and helped spread information about the political and economic conditions prevailing in India and China. Most of the information about contacts between China and India and the embassies sent by Indian rulers comes from Chinese sources. The first mention of south India and the Pallava capital Kanchi (though this identification is tentative) occurred in a work going back to the first century CE which noted that this region produced pearls and glass.[30] Buddhist travellers began to travel to India from the fifth century CE. Early in the sixth century, c. 510, a Chinese account mentioned an embassy to the Chinese court from south India which was described as the land of elephants and other wild animals, pearls, diamonds, brocaded muslins, aromatic plants, sugar cane and many other products.[31] The commodities listed demonstrated a keen interest in the prospects of trade between the two countries. The embassy sent to China in 720 CE by Rajasimha Pallava Narasimhavarman II is described only in the Chinese accounts.[32]

Intercourse between India and China had come to an end after the eighth century. The ninth century, which marked the last hundred years of the T'ang dynasty, was highly troubled and because of this the free passage of Buddhist travellers between China and India became almost non-existent. However, stability returned to China after the Song dynasty came to power in 960, which also revived political and commercial ties with India. Chinese histories recorded three embassies which were sent by the Chola kings to the Chinese emperor. The first was sent by Rajaraja I, 'Lo-tsa-lo-tsa' in the Chinese accounts, and reached the Chinese court in 1015, carrying a large quantity of pearls, ivory and frankincense.[33] A second embassy was sent by Rajendra I, 'Shi-lo-lo-cha Yin-to-lo-chulo', in 1033. Kulottunga I, 'Ti-hua-kia-lo', sent the third embassy, which reached China in 1077. The envoys carried glassware, camphor, brocades, rhinoceros horns, ivory, incense, spices and other expensive gifts for the Chinese emperor, and in return received a large amount of copper.[34]

Though the Chinese considered that all the Chola embassies were tributes from a subordinate ruler to their emperor, there is little doubt that the main aim of the Chola kings was to promote the trade interests of the Tamil merchants by making friendly overtures to the Chinese, especially in view of the fact that the sovereign position of China, both politically and economically, was acknowledged by all South-East Asian kingdoms. The interest of the Chola kings in maintaining good relations with China is further attested to by a stone inscription dated 1079 found in a Taoist monastery temple in Canton, which named the Chola king Kulottunga I as a most generous donor who had made a gift of 600,000 gold kasu to the temple.[35]

The Chinese accounts do not mention the active participation of Tamil (or Indian) merchants in the trade with India, leading earlier historians to infer that the trade in the Indian Ocean was controlled by Arabs and other sea-faring nations. However, the seventh of the Tamil inscriptions found in South-East Asia is of special interest in this context. This thirteenth-century inscription was discovered in Quanzhou, a famous medieval port of China, and refers to the construction of a Siva temple in the port. The temple was called Tirukkanichhuram, meaning the temple of the Khan after the Khan of China, one more instance of the Tamil custom of naming public places after the rulers. Many Hindu artefacts have been found in the area where the temple was located, and is a clear indication that a sizeable Tamil population had been living in Quanzhou at that time.[36] This also puts to rest the question raised by earlier historians as to whether there was any direct intercourse between China and Tamilakam during the early medieval period.

## Sailendra empire of Sri Vijaya

While the contacts of the Tamils with the kingdoms of South-East Asia were extensive, the Sri Vijaya kingdom under the Sailendra dynasty and Sri Lanka were of greater strategic importance, both politically and commercially, for Tamilakam. Overcoming the older Sri Vijaya kingdom of Sumatra, the Sailendras had built a great empire in the eighth century which extended from Java to Sumatra and covered the entire Malay Peninsula. The Chinese referred to the empire as San-fo-tsi, and contemporary Arab accounts called it Zabag or Zabaj. Their location and naval supremacy enabled the Sailendras to control the sea trade between China and West Asia. Ports on the Malay coast like Kedah, known as Kadaram in Tamil, in the medieval period, and Malacca in later centuries, were of crucial importance as entrepôts in the Indian Ocean trade and were also of strategic significance as control points in this trade.

Rajaraja I had cordial relations with the rulers of the Sailendra empire which was the greatest empire in South-East Asia. Because of this goodwill, the Sailendra emperor constructed a Buddhist *vihara* in the port of Nagapattinam, which took its name, Chudamanivihara, from his. Rajaraja granted a village for the upkeep of this vihara in 1006.[37] It has been argued that the construction of the vihara was an outcome of the growing trade between south India and South-East Asia, and the greater awareness in China of the importance of these trade links.[38]

The tenor of this relationship changed during the reign of Rajendra I who sent a naval force to attack Kadaram in 1017–18. In a campaign that lasted many years, the Chola forces captured Kadaram and many other cities, together with a great deal of treasure. The victory was described in detail in an inscription[39] and earned Rajendra I the title *kadaram konda*, conqueror of Kadaram. Historians have been unable to find a plausible reason which prompted the invasion, but most have concluded that this was undertaken to protect the commercial interests of Tamilakam which were perhaps threatened by the attempts of the Sailendra kings to monopolize the trade to the east because of their control over the ports of the Malay Peninsula. The expedition also yielded vast treasure and added glory to the emperor. Later Chola emperors of the eleventh century, Vira Rajendra and Kulottunga I, also claimed to have sent naval forces and captured Kadaram.[40]

Did the naval attacks by the Cholas change the contours of maritime trade and tilt it more in favour of Tamil merchants in the long run? Certainly, nothing really changed in political terms and the Sailendra kingdom of Sri Vijaya continued in strength until the thirteenth century when it was fully conquered by the king of Java. As seen earlier, the Sumatra inscription of the merchant guild, the Five Hundred, dating to the early eleventh century, is indicative of the presence of Tamil merchant groups operating in the ports. But whether the naval action by the Cholas resulted in a larger volume of trade for the Tamil merchants is open to question.

## Sri Lanka

Tamil relations with Sri Lanka were far more complex and highly volatile in terms of conflicts and political alliances. Prior to Chola rule, the Tamil kingdoms had invaded Sri Lanka several times. The Pallava kings Simhavishnu and Narasimhavarman I had sent naval forces to Sri Lanka, the latter to install Prince Manavarman of Sri Lanka on the throne, though he was deposed soon afterwards and sent into exile.[41] The Pandyan kings occasionally invaded Sri Lanka, but also formed alliances with the Sri Lankan rulers for support in their own conflicts with the Pallavas and Cholas. The great chronicle of Sri Lankan history, the *Mahavamsa*, has also recorded these political developments.[42]

The invasion of Sri Lanka by the Chola kings Rajaraja I and Rajendra I had much greater long-term significance. Rajaraja I invaded Sri Lanka in 993 and made northern Sri Lanka a province of the Chola empire. His forces destroyed Anuradhapura, the ancient capital, and shifted the capital further south to Polonnoruwa, in a move to establish Chola rule over the entire island.[43] Rajaraja's son and successor, Rajendra I completed the conquest of Sri Lanka in 1017–18. His inscriptions proclaimed that he had amassed a great amount of treasure during this conquest, a claim which is corroborated by the *Mahavamsa*, which described the looting of the island kingdom in more vivid detail.

In spite of such a comprehensive victory, the incorporation of Sri Lanka as a province of the Chola empire could not be sustained beyond a few years, and within twelve years Vikkamabahu had managed to free the southern part of the island from the invaders. The pattern of revolts by the Sri Lankans against the Cholas and retaliatory repression continued under Rajendra's sons and successors until Vijayabahu became the king of the entire kingdom in 1073 during the reign of Kulottunga I. The final postscript to Chola intervention in Sri Lanka happened in 1088, when Tamil mercenary soldiers known as *velaikkara* forces revolted against Vijayabahu, who put down the rebellion with brutal effectiveness.[44] The mercenaries gave an undertaking to serve the king loyally and the Buddhist shrine of

Polonnoruwa was placed under their protection. According to the *Mahavamsa*, the uprising was instigated by Kulottunga I who made a last-ditch attempt to restore Chola rule in Sri Lanka by exploiting the loyalty and sentiments of the very large Tamil population still living in the island.[45]

The Chola invasion and occupation of Sri Lanka were probably primarily motivated by dreams of imperial expansion. The inflow of a vast amount of treasure from the expeditions to Sri Vijaya and Sri Lanka would also have resulted in a considerable increase in the availability of capital within the Chola empire, which was used by the royal family and military elite for funding the construction and maintenance of temples.[46] It is not clear whether the promotion of the commercial interests of Tamil merchants was a secondary but major objective. Merchant communities and groups from south India had been active in the maritime trade between India, Sri Lanka and South-East Asia since the eighth century, mainly trading in aromatic woods, camphor, silk, porcelain and fine goods from South-East Asia and China.

At least fifteen inscriptions in Tamil have been discovered in Sri Lanka, mostly dated between 1100 and 1300, though two are dated as late as 1300 and 1400. Most of these inscriptions refer to the activities of the merchant guild, the Five Hundred or Nanadesi,[47] and it is evident that the commercial penetration of Sri Lanka by Tamil merchant groups survived much longer than the imperial expansion and occupation undertaken by the Cholas. One of the earliest inscriptions, dating to the eighth or ninth century, refers to a different merchant group called Nangunadu, of the four regions, who probably originated from Kerala and migrated to Anuradhapura because they were Buddhists. The inscription referred to a donation made by them to a Buddhist temple.

The Nanadesis migrated to Sri Lanka in large numbers following the Chola conquest, and gradually moved from the coastal areas in the north to form settlements further south in the interior. Their inscriptions are all dated after 1100, well after the Sri Lankan kings had managed to overthrow the Cholas and regain independence, which leads to the conclusion that the Tamil merchants had adapted themselves to changed conditions in Sri Lanka after Chola rule. The Nanadesis essentially replicated in Sri Lanka the traditional institutional arrangements which governed trading activities in Tamilakam. Their settlements developed into nagarams or market centres, and the administration and affairs of the nagaram were managed by a corporate assembly referred to in the Sri Lankan inscriptions as *perumakkal*, the great people. Corporate assemblies managed all local resources and administration in Tamilakam, and the same practice was followed in Sri Lanka. In fact, Anuradhapura was known as *perur*, the great town, along the same lines as the managaram in Tamilakam.

In Sri Lanka, as in Tamilakam, the term Nanadesi or Five Hundred did not denote a homogeneous group of merchants. Rather, it was an umbrella term referring to an organization which comprised many trading communities, soldiers and artisans. The Nanadesis also continued to use other epithets which they commonly used in Tamilakam to refer to themselves, like *padinenvishayam* (the origin of this term is not clear; it meant, of the eighteen regions). In Sri Lanka too, as in their homeland, they had armed soldiers to protect their caravans, and often honoured these soldiers by naming the town as *eriviratanam*, known as *erivirapattanam* in Tamilakam, which literally meant the place or town of the warrior.

While the Nanadesis retained the traditional institutional structures in the manner in which they operated in Tamilakam, they also acclimatized themselves to the different ground realities in Sri Lanka. This mainly took the form of supporting Buddhist temples and institutions through donations, which was important in a Buddhist country. At the request of Lilavati, queen of King Parakramabahu I, they funded an almshouse for Buddhist pilgrims who visited Anuradhapura. This highlights the fact that the Nanadesis were prosperous merchants who were recognized and held in high esteem by local society and who could be approached for charitable donations. Yet, they themselves continued to be Hindus which is proven by the remains of Hindu temples and bronze icons which have been excavated from their settlements.

## Tamil merchants in South-east Asia and Sri Lanka: A study in responses

It is instructive to conclude this section with a brief account of the lives of Tamil merchants in South-East Asia and Sri Lanka. All over the world, maritime merchants usually had to sojourn for long periods in foreign ports during the ancient and medieval periods because of the wind patterns and weather conditions that governed sea-borne trade. Similarly, the Tamil merchants also had to stay in ports of South-East Asia for long periods. This provides a basis for understanding the behaviour of migrant merchant groups. Inscriptions from all over South-East Asia corroborate that Tamil merchants had their own settlements in many ports across the region in the medieval period. These inscriptions date back to the ninth century, but in all probability the merchant settlements had actually been established several centuries earlier. These continued well into the thirteenth century and later, and were still active and in evidence when the European trading companies began to participate in Indian Ocean trade after the fifteenth century.

There was probably little tension or contradiction between local and migrant culture and values in South-East Asia because countries across the entire region had been ruled by Hindu kings originating from India since the fourth century CE, and Hindu culture had permeated into these societies as a result of the close contact which was maintained with India over many centuries. Even Buddhism was not an alien religion to the Indian merchants, and the spread of Buddhism did not create a hostile environment. The Tamil merchants therefore concentrated primarily on creating public facilities for their own community. The inscriptions confirm that Tamil merchants had constructed Hindu temples and other structures like temple tanks and halls, all to serve their own community in South-East Asian cities.

The situation in Sri Lanka after the eleventh century was more complex. Sri Lanka had had a long, tortuous and conflict-ridden relationship with the Tamil kingdoms over many centuries. This was further complicated after the invasion and conquest of the country by the Chola kings, and it can be inferred that tensions still marred the relations between the Tamils and the local Sinhalese even after the Cholas were forced to withdraw from the island. The revolt of the armed Tamil mercenaries who continued in Sri Lanka against the king is just one case in point. The Tamil merchant community of the Nanadesis was active in Sri Lanka for more than 300 years after the eleventh century, which would lead to the inference that commerce could function in an unfavourable political climate. The Tamil merchant groups recreated in Sri Lanka the same institutions and organizational structures in which they functioned in Tamilakam. Although they maintained their cultural identity by constructing Hindu temples, they also made a conscious effort to respond to the sensitivities of the Sri Lankan people by donating liberally to Buddhist temples and charities with even the queen approaching them to support a religious charity for Buddhist pilgrims. The merchant community thus effectively achieved a balance between their need to retain their own identity while gaining recognition from the authorities of the host society.

# 4. THE TEMPLE, NAGARAM AND MERCHANTS: A STUDY IN SYNERGY

THE TEMPLE EMERGED as the central, definitive institution in south India after the sixth century. It energized social and economic processes in Tamilakam setting in motion a complex set of interactions between the rulers and local institutions, between urban and rural settlements, and between merchants and corporate bodies because the temple became an institution which represented a synthesized value system combining religious merit, social control and economic power.

## THE REVIVAL OF THE TEMPLE

Hindu temples had fallen into a state of decay when Jainism and Buddhism became the dominant religions in the Tamil region. The bhakti movement which began in the late sixth and early seventh centuries signalled the revival of Hinduism in the Tamil region. According to popular tradition, based on the hagiographic account of the sixty-three saints of Saivism, Tirunavukkarasar, the first of the Saivite saints, is depicted with a small spade in his hand which he used to clear the weeds and undergrowth in the untended outer yards of temples, symbolizing the movement to renovate and revitalize the temples by motivating the local people to become involved in his efforts.

Temple construction was undertaken at an increasing pace after the Pallava and Pandya kings reconverted to Hinduism under the influence of the early Saivite saints. As the Chola empire grew in power and size, there was a great increase in the construction of new temples across the region,[1] perhaps in fulfilment of the Tamil dictum that every settlement should have a temple. The modes and technology of temple construction also underwent major changes during this period. The first was the transition from rock-cut architecture to structural stone temples under the Pallavas. This was significant in terms of the design and economics of temple construction. Temples were no longer limited in size by the dimensions of rocks as in the case of rock-cut structures. With advancing technical knowledge it became possible to construct larger temples which were increasingly built by the Cholas; they reached their zenith in Rajarajesvaram, the 'big temple' as it is known even today, built by Rajaraja I in Tanjavur, and its replica built by Rajendra I in Gangaikondacholapuram. Larger temples also catered to larger congregations, offering more religious services, which in turn called for greater resources and stronger management.

Large temples became feasible because the economy was expanding and commerce was flourishing in the Chola period. Temple complexes with many sanctums came up which also promoted cultural, educational and other social services.[2] For instance, the formal, inaugural presentation of the great Tamil work Kamban's *Ramayanam* was done in the temple at Srirangam, while Sekkilar's history of the Saivite saints, the *Periyapuranam*, was first presented in the presence of the king in the temple at Chidambaram. Public performances of dance and music were held in the temple courtyard or dance halls, especially during the major temple festivals, so that the temple became the institution which promoted all performing arts.

## The temple as a social institution

During this period the temple underwent a metamorphosis from a mono-functional religious institution which catered to the spiritual needs of the people to an institution of multiple and complex functions. Temples were mostly constructed by kings and other members of the royal family. This in itself served many objectives, in addition to the most visible one of gaining *punniyam*, religious merit. Temple building gave increased legitimacy to the king in terms of public opinion as the rightful and acknowledged ruler of the land who upheld accepted principles of dharma or moral values. As in the case of endowing brahmadeya villages through land assignments to Brahmins, the construction of temples strengthened the position of the reigning families in the region.

Once consecrated, temples had to function effectively providing a variety of ritual services to the local people. This required resources on a large scale which were raised through donations of land, livestock and money. Donors primarily came from local propertied classes and their gifting earned them both religious merit and recognition in local society which cemented their social and economic status. This also ensured that the local elite who led the corporate assemblies could be in charge of the management of the affairs and resources of the temple, which was a position of great prestige and honour.

The significance of the temple, however, went much

beyond this. In a reflection of its centrality, the temple became the depository of all information relating to administration and resource management. Temple inscriptions were not just records of donations and decisions relating to the management of the temple. In the absence of detailed and authoritative histories like the *Mahavamsa* of Sir Lanka, inscriptions constitute the most comprehensive source of information for the reconstruction of political, economic and social history of the medieval period. Inscriptions generally began with an introductory eulogy known as *prasasti* or *meykirtti* of the ruling king which recorded his military conquests. The victories of Rajaraja I and of Rajendra I in Kadaram and Sri Lanka are described only in the meykirttis of contemporary inscriptions which therefore have been the main source of historical information for the period. Inscriptions also give details of the functioning of local assemblies and administration; of revenue assessment and taxation; of the management and more productive use of land and irrigation resources through reclamation, desilting, repairing sluices and building of embankments.

Beyond all this, the temple was a public forum where a variety of extraneous, unrelated information was also recorded. For instance, a tenth century inscription from Tanjavur district states that a Brahmin had gifted land to his second wife,[3] which raises many conjectures as to

Figure 4.1 Inscriptions from the Tanjavur Temple, Rajarajesvaram
(from personal collection)

why a purely private, intra-household disposal of assets
needed to be recorded in a public institution. At the
other end of the spectrum, a thirteenth century
inscription from North Arcot district was a statement
by all sections of local society comprising the nattar,
military leaders, wage workers, migrants from Malayala
country, merchants, Paraiyar or dalits and their leaders,
cobblers and Irulas or tribals that they did not accept the
current rulers who were 'usurpers' and that they would
only accept the sons of the legitimate wife of the king as
their ruler.[4] Thus, for more than three centuries, over a

period which saw the rise and ultimate disintegration of the powerful Chola empire, the position of the temple remained stable, and it retained its significance as the focal point of social interaction and an outlet for the concerns of the community. It is because of this that the subsequent analysis of the functioning of trade and the economy is seen through the prism of the temple.

## TEMPLES AND THE ECONOMY

The economic ramifications of the temple were many. The construction of a temple in itself was a major public enterprise. As most temples were built by kings or members of the royal family, temple building involved a great deal of public expenditure. Construction activity also created employment on a large scale for skilled masons, sculptors and craftsmen, as also for unskilled labour. The custom of installing bronze icons in the temple which were taken out in processions led to the development of a huge craft industry in bronze casting and metal work. In fact, to this day, the region around Tanjavur and Kumbakonam has a large number of craftsmen creating artefacts in bronze and brass. The multiplier effects of this expansion of employment and earnings would have been significant, though they cannot be quantified with certainty.

## The temple as an economic entity[5]

The temple required considerable resources to discharge all its functions effectively. In all activities, the temple or, more accurately, the presiding deity of the temple was deemed to be a person in a legal sense, and all transactions were carried out in the name of the deity. The temple was an employer on a large scale since it needed priests who were well versed in rituals and scriptures to perform pujas and conduct ceremonies; cooks and other staff to manage the temple kitchens; dancing girls and musicians to perform in the temple; and a host of workers to keep the temple functioning. Priests and dancing girls were usually paid through assignment of land, while workers were paid in paddy from the lands owned by the temple itself.

The temple was also a major consumer of basic commodities like oil or ghee to keep the temple lamps burning. Every temple had lamps which burned day and night continuously known as *nonda vilakku*, as well as lamps which were lit in the morning and at dusk, *sandhyadipam*. In addition, the temple needed rice, lentils, seasonings, spices and fruits like bananas for the daily offerings of food. Flowers used to decorate the icons formed an important requirement. The temple also required a variety of high-value aromatic substances like camphor, musk, rosewater, saffron and sandalwood, many of which were imported, to be used in the ritual baths and paste applications for the icons. For instance, a donor in Tanjavur in the eleventh century specified that the interest on his donation should be used to supply cardamom and *champaka* buds, a fragrant flower, for the ritual bathwater in the temple.[6] The temple thus played multiple economic roles as an employer and as a consumer, which have been noted by many historians.[7]

Temples therefore needed substantial monetary resources for their everyday basic functions in addition to carrying out a variety of ritual services which were particularly expected of bigger temples by the devotees. The latter was extremely important for the survival of the temple since, if the devotees stopped frequenting the temple, its resources would diminish and it would not be possible to sustain the temple. Required resources were raised almost entirely through donations of land, livestock and money from all sections of society—royalty, military leaders, corporate assemblies, merchants and individual donors, and from the income earned through the disposal of these donations.

## Temples and land grants

Donations of land to temples were made under various terms and conditions. In certain cases, the temples had proprietary rights over the land, which meant that they could lease it out to whomever they chose as a tenant. On lands given as *devadana*, gifted to God, temples were landholders and had superior rights to the produce of the land from the tenant cultivators, but could not change the tenancy arrangements at will. Some lands were gifted as *iraiyili*, tax-free; on some lands the kings assigned the taxes due to the state to the temple. But in many cases, the taxes on the donated lands were paid to the state by the donors themselves, so that there was little diminution of state revenue.

Land donations were made not merely because they earned religious merit for the donors. Though this was the overt stated objective, it has been pointed out that this practice also had an economic objective of expanding agriculture and increasing production by bringing more land under cultivation. The Tirupati temple, the richest temple in south India, utilized its land grants and donations of money interactively for bringing more land under irrigation, especially during the Vijayanagar period, which in turn increased the productivity of land and the supply of food grains to the temple. The food grains were used to prepare consecrated food offerings which were sold to the devotees, providing an important source of income to the temple.[8]

It is not clear whether the same dynamics were in operation in the Chola heartland. There is no evidence that consecrated food offerings were sold to the devotees as was the practice in Tirupati. More importantly, compared to the region around Tirupati which was, and continues to be, deficient in rain and water resources, the river basins of southern Tamilakam were already fully developed and irrigated by the eleventh century, under the aggressive revenue and agrarian administration of the Cholas. However, land often became uncultivable due to river flooding and silting. An inscription of the Srirangam temple, now a part of the city of Tiruchi, dating to 1022 stated that the temple gifted such land to two merchants who had reclaimed it, removing the silt and building embankments, so that they were able to grow paddy and sugar cane. In return, they and their heirs would supply *aval*, beaten rice, in perpetuity to the temple.[9] Similarly, lands donated to the temples were brought under cultivation through reclamation, in addition to leasing out lands which had reverted as village commons for a variety of reasons.[10] This was one more instance of how the temple combined practical and material considerations under the overtly stated objectives of spiritual merit and religious charity.

## Temple donations and capital formation

Donations to temples comprised a variety of immovable and movable assets: land, livestock—cattle or sheep—

and money or gold. Land donations primarily provided temples with paddy which was used to pay the wages of the temple employees and to prepare food offerings in daily temple rituals. Food was also provided to visiting pilgrims and devotees, and donations made for this purpose spelt out in great detail the items to be served: one donation specified that there should be rice, three vegetables, salt, buttermilk and ghee, ending with four betel leaves and two areca nuts. The donation also included the cost of pots and pans and fuel.[11] Donated land was also used to create gardens to supply flowers to the temple. Cattle or sheep were donated to provide ghee for the temple lamps. Money was donated for many specified purposes, which included ornaments for the icons, oil for lamps and food offerings.

Land which was donated was generally used directly by the temple. But land was also sold to the temple which usually involved multilateral transactions, especially when the land belonged to the assembly of the nagaram. The sequence of transactions began with the sale of land to the temple by the nagaram. From the proceeds realized, the nagaram agreed to remit the taxes due on the land so that the temple would possess the land free of the burden of taxes. The money realized from the sale was evidently used as capital for more productive or commercial ventures by the nagaram—

though this is not actually recorded—and the land tax would be paid from the interest or profits earned on this capital.[12] When land was sold to individuals by the nagaram, the same sequence of transactions was adopted, though often the buyers would later gift the land to the temple.

Donations for oil or ghee for burning lamps in the temple were paid directly to shepherds or oil mongers. Livestock was donated in herds of thirty-two cows and a bull, or a herd of ninety-six sheep comprising ewes and rams,[13] so that the herd could be propagated in perpetuity. In the colourful terminology of the inscriptions, the herd 'would neither age nor die'! These herds were deemed sufficient to supply enough ghee for the temple lamps and were given to the *manradiar* or *idaiyar*, shepherds, who undertook to supply ghee to the temple each day for the lamps. One *uri*[14] of ghee was considered enough for a lamp to burn throughout the day, and this was in effect the interest on the capital which was transferred to the shepherds. Often, the corporate assemblies, the nagaram or sabha, borrowed money from the temple and agreed to supply the required amount of ghee or oil as interest on the money. It is evident that individual donors as well as the temple authorities preferred to give the donation to corporate groups since a collective body was perceived as better security. It has been observed that the temple authorities were not interested in the question of who possessed the asset; they wanted to be assured of the supply of ghee, oil and other commodities which would enable the daily services of the temple to continue uninterrupted.[15]

Money was also deposited directly with the nagaram or sabha which undertook to supply the ghee or oil for the temple lamps. Often there was a stipulation in the recording of the donation that the money was under the *rakshai*, protection, of the nagaram or sabha. Merchant guilds like the Five Hundred were also entrusted with donations. The risk of default of payment by individual borrowers was deemed high and a larger group or nagaram would undertake to be guarantor for the loan. The shepherds of the temple in Melpadi, North Arcot, as a collective body thus stood security for ninety sheep received by one shepherd. Similarly, the Sivapuram nagaram of Kilur, South Arcot district, jointly signed an agreement when three member merchants borrowed money to supply turmeric to the temple to be used for turmeric paste or *manjal kappu*.[16]

The inscriptions display remarkable consistency and stability in these arrangements from the ninth till the thirteenth century. Perhaps the only change worth noting is the increasing role of itinerant merchant guilds which are mentioned with much greater frequency in inscriptions after the twelfth century.

## Business practices: Interest rates and monetization

Temples provided the ideal institutional base for capital formation as well as the circulation of capital across various sections of society. Endowments to the temple comprised donations and deposits. In the case of deposits, the purpose was mentioned. Money was deposited as *nilai poliyuttu*, a permanent deposit, though it is not clear if the deposit was expected to be repaid. Business concepts of interest or *palisai* as the income on capital and credit were well understood even before the ninth century. More than a dozen inscriptions dating to the eighth and ninth centuries give details of interest to be paid on donations, both in money and in kind.[17]

Interest rates were nearly always specified. Interest could be paid as a percentage on the borrowed capital, or in kind, which meant that the return was calculated based on the price of the commodity to be supplied in lieu of interest. Since an overwhelming majority of donations were intended for temple lamps, the interest had to be paid in ghee or oil; in rice, dal and ghee for cooked food; flowers; turmeric or fragrant substances and spices, used in ceremonial baths. Interest was sometimes also defined as service. In the eighth century, the *ganam*, local assembly, of Paiyanur, Chengalpattu district, agreed to remove the silt from the large tank in the village each year as interest on paddy given by a merchant of Mamallapuram.[18]

Non-specific gifts of gold or money were lent out on interest by the temple. According to a tenth-century inscription, the temple of Tiruvoṟṟiyur, now a northern suburb of Chennai, invested a part of 60 *kalañju* gold which it had been gifted with the residents of a village near Ponneri, further north, at an interest of 15 per cent, payable every six months, including two meals for the man who went to collect the interest from the borrowers.[19]

Interest rates generally ranged between 12.5 and 15 per cent a year, but could vary between a low of 6.25 per cent and a high of 30 per cent a year. What factors governed the determination of interest rates? It is difficult to even hazard a guess as to whether this was due to local conditions which indicated increased risk or insufficient resources for credit, since donations and deposits were being made to temples throughout the entire region. An eleventh-century inscription gives a clear idea that there was an active functioning credit market. It refers to merchants from outside the locality and local merchants whose business was lending money on interest.[20] Since the interest rate essentially represented the cost of capital, profits made on transactions using this capital had to be more than the interest rate for the activity to be viable.

To what extent was the economy functioning as a money economy? This again can only be conjectured. We observe that money or gold coins are often mentioned and taxes were paid both in paddy and in cash. Many donations also specify the amount in terms of money. The introduction of gold and silver coins during the Chola period indicates a higher level of prosperity and economic development compared to the Pallava period when the coins were of lead or copper. Gold coins—kalanju and kasu—were in circulation, in addition to coins of a lower denomination like *manjadi*. The equivalents were not uniform, but as a rule of thumb 8 manjadi was equal to 1 kasu, and 2 kasu made 1 kalanju.[21] In addition to these coins, there is also mention of *ilakkasu*, presumably a gold coin from Sri Lanka, which was in circulation. The kalanju was a gold weight of 80 grains. Donations of gold also use the terms *tulaippon* or *sempon* to indicate gold of the best purity. Gold and coins were usually mentioned as interchangeable units. However, wages to agricultural labourers and temple staff were paid in paddy, and it would be safe to say that the economy functioned for the most part on barter with paddy as the medium of exchange.

Figure 4.2 Coins of Rajaraja, Rajendra Gangaikondacholan and Kulottunga

## Capital and redistribution

The manner in which donations were utilized by the temple led to the circulation and redistribution of resources across a wide cross-section of society which made for a more inclusive and growth-oriented economy. The degree to which this resulted in more equitable distribution depended on the class composition of the donors and of the borrowers. Not much redistribution was possible in the case of land donations since existing tenancy arrangements were often not disturbed and agrarian relations continued without much change. Livestock however was redistributed among a large number of shepherds creating capital assets for the less-privileged sections of agrarian society.

The Rajarajesvaram temple built by Rajaraja I in Tanjavur becomes a special case for studying the redistributive aspects of a temple. Donations to the temple were of two categories—livestock and money. Most of the livestock was donated by the king and nobility (69.3 per cent of the cows and 98.3 per cent of the ewes). Military officers were the main donors of money, accounting for 79.3 per cent of all donations. Livestock was better redistributed since cattle or sheep rearing was done only by shepherds as an occupational group. Money, however, was borrowed almost exclusively by village assemblies (95.4 per cent). Presumably, this money was circulated in the local rural economy and used for the development of agriculture. Merchants were the other category of borrowers (4.6 per cent). One hypothesis offered is that the donations of the nobility and the military transferred the treasure and livestock captured in the military conquests of the Chola army to the temple. For the donor, this gained religious merit and, perhaps more importantly, political advantage since the Tanjavur temple was a project close to the heart of Rajaraja.[22]

Clearly, such conclusions based on a study of only one temple with royal patronage have only limited applicability and cannot be generalized for the functioning of all temples. This is particularly valid with reference to the role of the military. My earlier work covering a larger cross-section of temples in Tamil Nadu also shows that corporate bodies—ur, sabha, nagaram and guild—greatly outnumbered individual merchants as borrowers of donations made to temples. Individual merchants, on the other hand, constituted 56 per cent of the donors (in my sample). Royalty, officials and the military were relatively few and accounted for a very small proportion of the donors.[23]

In sum, temples became the vehicle for mobilizing the economic surplus which they received through donations and deposits and utilizing and transforming the resources into productive capital in both the agrarian and urban economy.

## NAGARAM, TEMPLES AND URBANIZATION

Urbanization was the key factor in the expansion of commerce. In medieval Tamilakam, this process was closely linked to the growth of temples. As we have already noted with reference to the temples in Tiruvallikkeni and Kanchipuram, even as early as the eighth century the areas surrounding temples were developed as townships by the kings. Under the Cholas, temple building and urbanization gained momentum with the construction of several large temples and temple complexes comprising many shrines. The multiple economic roles played by temples as employers, landowners and consumers of goods and services necessarily also involved exchange, leading to the development of towns and the expansion of commerce.

As the corporate assembly of the town, the nagaram was primarily concerned with the urban economy and trading activities inasmuch that its membership comprised the local merchant groups. However, it should be remembered that the medieval economy was characterized not by rural–urban dichotomy but by rural–urban continuum, so much so that nagarams were also involved in the management of agricultural land. For instance, nagarams, like the village assemblies, were responsible for the collection of land revenue from the agricultural land in the hinterland of towns which was under their jurisdiction.[24] In fact, nagarams even donated land to temples throughout the Chola period. On many occasions, the land sold was later gifted to the temples. There is, however, no mention of nagarams buying land, which is perhaps an indication that they were more oriented to the management of urban affairs and trade.

Because of the long continuities in south Indian history, historians often tend to treat the four centuries from the mid ninth century to the mid thirteenth as a homogeneous period when no major changes took place. But a more nuanced approach would be to discern the inter-temporal dynamics of urbanization under the Cholas. Before the ninth century, only four nagarams were mentioned in Pallava inscriptions and Mamallapuram, the main port, and Kanchipuram, the capital, were designated as managaram. There was significant growth in the number of nagarams during the reigns of the great Chola emperors, Rajaraja I, Rajendra I and Kulottunga I (985–1150), throughout the Chola heartland and also in regions assimilated into the Chola empire through conquest, reflecting the accelerated pace of urban development and inter-regional trade.[25] Nagarams had spread as far north as Visakhapatnam by the late twelfth century,[26] no doubt due to the incorporation of the region in the Chola empire under the later Cholas. After the twelfth century, more nagarams came up further south when Pandya rule was re-established.

The importance of trade and merchants was recognized by the ruling classes, who actively promoted trade by offering incentives to merchants to settle in or to return to a locality. The local official of

Tirunamanallur, South Arcot district, in 1154 invited member merchants of the local nagaram who had migrated to other places to return and settle once again in the town.[27] Similarly, in 1250, the local chief of Chidambaram granted about 4.3 *veli* of land (about 11 hectares) to create a new hamlet as a nagaram for the Saliyar or weavers.[28]

## Nagaram

The nagaram was a corporate institution and a specialized commercial centre.[29] How did the commercial activities in a nagaram differ from village-level exchange? One difference would be that in a village exchange was governed by patron–client relationships and service providers dealt with the community in return for a share in the village produce, a social system which in current terminology is referred to as *jajmani*. In towns, however, trade was carried on between sellers of goods and services and buyers on the basis of market exchange. It has been observed that there was one nagaram in each nadu, acting as the marketing centre for the agrarian hinterland. The nagaram was the link in a hierarchy of markets, linking the villages to the market town, which was linked to higher order centres like the managaram and port towns. The authority of the nagaram over local trade and markets is indicated by the fact that the nagaram collected taxes on all commercial transactions and fees from commercial services. It also provided the functions of a city government, such as police protection, street cleaning and so on. On the whole, while there was one nagaram in each nadu which was the central marketing centre for the agricultural hinterland, there were instances of more than one nagaram in a nadu.[30] A curious exception was Tanjavur, the Chola capital, where four nagarams were listed in the outer suburbs of the city.[31] These nagarams were probably established by royal fiat to serve the expanding capital city of the empire.

The nagaram was also about the physical structures that constituted the market. Unlike the aspatial, abstract markets of economic theory, real-life markets function in space with a hierarchy of structures. Thus, in the nagaram there were *kadai*, shops, *angadi*, markets or bazaars, and the *perangadi*, big market in the inner city, which perhaps was the wholesale market. The shops and markets were located on streets in the market zone which were referred to as *perunteru*, big or main streets. The nagaram was always associated with the big street, and always referred to as 'the nagaram of such and such big street'. To this day one can find a 'big street' in the central zone of most old cities in Tamil Nadu. The hierarchy of structures evokes a vivid, visual picture of streets bustling with buyers and vendors, trading from shops on the main market streets. The mention of a market as distinct from a shop indicates that areas were demarcated for trade in different commodities. This pattern of markets and trading can be seen even today in all major temple towns where the roads leading to the temple are lined with shops buzzing with traders and buyers.

A point of interest and curiosity for a contemporary social scientist was the habit of naming towns and streets after the kings and queens. In the Chola period, the names and titles of the great Cholas, especially of Rajaraja I and Rajendra I like *nigarilicholan*, the incomparable Chola, *mummudi cholan*, the thrice crowned Chola, Arulmolideva (the given name of Rajaraja) and of the queens, Tribhuvanamadevi, Vanavanmadevi or Lokamadevi, were repeatedly used for streets and towns. Interestingly, even merchants occasionally took these titles. According to an inscription of 1034, the merchants of Kalahasti in Chittoor district even added titles like *kadaram konda cholan*, the title of Rajendra I, or the names Uttama Chola, Karikala Chola and Rajendra Chola to their given names.[32]

The nagaram was strictly an institution which governed local trade. Its functions related to the management of local merchants and markets, agricultural land, temples and collection of taxes. On what terms did it interact with itinerant merchants and merchant groups like the guilds? In all probability, itinerant merchants or groups who brought in commodities which were not locally produced dealt only with the merchants of the nagaram. The exchange was therefore conducted like wholesale trade between the merchants, while direct transactions with the local buyers were the prerogative of local merchants. Among the latter, some were also authorized to act as sole brokers or agents to supply local products to the itinerant merchants.[33]

The membership of a nagaram was very broad-based and included all local residents, as in a sabha or ur. The most comprehensive list of members comes from an inscription of Chidambaram dating to the eleventh century in the reign of Rajendra I. The members of the local nagaram known as Gunamenagaipuram comprised the merchants, the Vellala landowners, Sankarappadi or oil merchants, saliyar or weavers and fishermen who were residents or citizens of the town, and lower order artisans like carpenters, masons, goldsmiths and leather workers.[34] Invariably, all the local merchants were named *chetti* or *mayilatti*. In this context, the term chetti should be taken as a generic term for merchants and not as a caste appellation that it came to denote by the seventeenth century.

There were two communities of oil mongers—Sankarappadi and Vaniyar. The distinction between the two was probably based on caste ranking, and the Sankarappadi claimed a higher ritual status in the caste hierarchy.[35] The Sankarappadi were referred to as a nagaram, *Sankarappadi-nagarattar*, even in the tenth century,[36] and was the first of the occupational nagarams. The other such specialized nagarams made their appearance only in the twelfth century. Saliyar, the weavers, were earlier mentioned among the many constituents of the nagaram; from the twelfth century, there are references to *Saliya nagaram/nagarattar*. The Vaniyar also became a nagaram in their own right in the thirteenth century, though they were mentioned only as constituent members of the nagaram even in the late eleventh century.[37] Such changes indicated a stage when there was a qualitative change in the development of the nagaram, and there was increased specialization in marketing which gave rise to these specialized nagarams.[38]

The basic information leaves many unanswered questions. Was there a formal process through which these groups attained the status of nagarams? How much autonomy did the occupational group nagarams enjoy within the overarching jurisdiction of the nagaram? This is not clear. They evidently dealt primarily with their own concerns as producers who were also traders. The Sankarappadi and Vaniya nagarams committed themselves only to supplying oil to the temples, either as donations or as interest against assignments of land or money made by other donors. The Saliya nagarams, on the other hand, evidently had jurisdiction over agricultural land, which they donated to temples.[39] New specialized nagarams were coming up even as late as the fourteenth century. In 1346, in Coimbatore district, there was a reference to a nagaram calling itself the *vaisya-vaniyar.* The members introduced themselves with a glowing eulogy about their antecedents, and followed this with a list of taxes that they assigned to the temple,[40] all of which indicates a high degree of autonomy in the functioning of these nagarams.

The emphasis on the nagaram as an institution of trade overshadows the economic importance of cities as centres of production. Urban streets were always segregated by occupation, and every city or town had a *saliyar teru,* weavers' street.[41] Kanchipuram continued to be designated a managaram even in the twelfth century, long after it had lost its political importance as the Pallava capital, mainly because of its continued significance as a manufacturing centre. The Madras Museum copper plates of the tenth century describe the city centre of Kanchipuram during the reign of Uttama

Chola.[42] Two classes of silk weavers, the Pattusali, lived in four quarters of the city and wove cloth for the king; some of them were appointed managers of the temple who had the responsibility of writing the accounts of the temple, an indication of their importance. Weaving and metal work which had no backward linkages to agriculture were the main city-based production activities. Cloth was a commodity which featured prominently in internal trade and was also a major item of export from the region.

In addition to its role as a marketing institution, the nagaram was actively involved in the administration of temples. However, there is little evidence of the involvement of the nagaram in the administration of the Rajarajesvaram temple in Tanjavur, or the other important temples in Srirangam or Tirupati. The traditional institutions were thus marginalized in great temple centres which developed under royal patronage.[43] Nagarams, however, did actively control the administration of many other temples across the region. The large temple complex of Tiruvidaimarudur, near Tanjavur, dedicated to Siva was a notable example. The Tiruvidaimarudur temple was administered by the sabha of 300 members, the nagaram which had 400 members, the *devakarmi*, temple officials, and *srikaryam arayginra*, an official who supervised the functioning of the temple.

The local ur is mentioned only once as part of the governing group, and was clearly much less important than the sabha. This administrative arrangement functioned with remarkable stability in Tiruvidaimarudur over more than 200 years from the tenth till the twelfth century.

The duties of temple administrators were partly ceremonial and partly functional. As a large temple situated close to the capital city of Tanjavur, the Tiruvidaimarudur temple was regularly patronized by royalty. All the administrators were present whenever the queen visited the temple, or when a large gift was made, for instance, when the queen donated a gold icon weighing 1172 kalanju.[44] Similarly, they assembled when their presence was required, both as a ceremonial formality and as a legal requirement, to be witnesses on occasions when a royal order was issued or when gifts of land and sheep were made, an indication of the meticulous procedures governing all transactions taking place in a temple.

The most important aspect of temple management was the strict maintaining of accounts of the deposits and donations made to the temple and their utilization. The sabha, nagaram and officials usually met in the dancing hall of the temple to decide on all financial matters, as well as to decide about other temple activities like the arrangement of dance performances. In a curious instance of arbitrariness, the sabha and nagaram decided to divert gold which had been donated for digging a tank and used it for making a gold chain, which for self-glorification was named the 'seven hundred' in their own honour, since they were 700 in number.[45] Temple finances and functioning were carefully audited by the srikaryam or supervising official to prevent malfeasance and misuse of funds. A fine was imposed on the management when it was deemed fit, as happened when three nagarattar of the Tillaisthanam temple in Tanjavur district were found guilty of mismanagement of temple funds.[46]

The responsibility of the nagaram for collecting taxes which had to be remitted to the state treasury has already been noted. All commodities traded by volume or weight, all professions, implements used in production like looms and oil presses, and other services were all covered in the tax net. Nagarams also raised resources by taxing themselves and assigning the proceeds to the temple. In 1080, military chiefs and the nagarattar of three streets in Nellore decided that they would pay a tax on the tolls levied on all weighed and measured goods, and also levy a cess on the families of the bride and groom during all weddings.[47] Similar undertakings were recorded many times. Goods on which taxes would be paid included cloth, pepper, areca nut, yarn, salt, grains and horses which indicates the extent and diversified nature of interregional trade.[48]

After the twelfth century, the nagarams made agreements jointly with merchant guilds to pay taxes on goods which were being sold locally, or even when they were merely in transit.[49] The importance of the merchant guild was clearly on the ascendant from the twelfth century and nagarams were associating themselves with the guilds, an evidence of a reorientation of the relative positions of institutions. This perhaps was the factor which ensured the continued survival of the nagaram well into the sixteenth century even as agrarian institutions like the nadu, sabha and ur faded away under Vijayanagar rule. In 1521, the nagarattar and leaders of merchant guilds of various towns decided to provide money to build two pavilions in the temple at Nagalapuram (Chengalpattu district) by collecting a cess from each house as also tolls on cloth and other goods exported by ship from Pulicat and other coastal towns.[50] An even later inscription from Kalahasti (Chittoor district) also mentions the nagaram,[51] both showing that nagarams were still active and relevant.

# MERCHANTS AND MERCHANT GUILDS

## Individual Merchants

Merchants in general, apart from being members of the larger corporate body, the nagaram, were also prominent players as individuals in an economic and social environment which favoured collective institutions. They made donations to temples in their own names as individuals, while they also recorded their collective identity as members of their nagaram,[52] perhaps to indicate that the donations were being made with the concurrence of the nagaram. While trade was clearly their main economic activity, merchants were also into transactions in land: buying, selling, donating and reclaiming land, which again reinforces the earlier observation that the economy was characterized by rural–urban continuum.

Taken across the region as a whole, individual merchants outnumbered all other donors to temples between the ninth and the thirteenth century, accounting for 56 per cent of all donors, though they constituted a very small percentage of borrowers from temple funds and deposits.[53] Most merchants made small donations of two to three kalanjus though several merchants made significantly larger donations. In the tenth and the eleventh centuries, donations of even ten kalanju would be considered large donations. Two very large donations stand out. In the tenth century, two brothers who were merchants donated 20.5 veli and 1 ma of land to the temple towards feeding 100 people each day, and also paid 300 kalanju gold as the fee for reclaiming the land they had bought from the sabha.[54] In another instance, in the eleventh century, a merchant of Srirangam bought two plots of land with fruit trees and a well for 20,000 kasu, which he endowed for a flower garden from which nine garlands would be supplied to the temple each day.[55]

In general, donations of larger magnitude usually ranged between 30 and 35 kalanjus. We must look at relative prices in order to put the value of these donations in perspective. In the eleventh century, the average output of 1 veli of land was 100 or 102 *kalam*s of paddy, and 1 veli was equal to 2.67 hectares or 6.4 acres. It is difficult to give a meaningful equivalent for a kalam, but it was a relatively large volumetric measure. Paddy sold for 8 kalams for 1 kasu or half a kalanju. Thus the value of the produce of 1 veli was between 12.5 and 12.75 kasu; a donation of 30 kalanju represented the value of the produce of more than 4.5 veli or 11.5 hectares of land.

There was a conspicuous increase in the value of the larger donations after the twelfth century when the larger donations amounted to between 70 and 80 kalanju.

There were two donations of more than 1000 kasu,[56] and a singularly large gift of gold and silver jewellery (57 kalanju gold and 85 kalanju silver) by a merchant to the temple at Vedaranyam, Tanjavur district.[57] The higher value of donations clearly points to the expansion of trade and economic activity in the region in the twelfth century as compared to two centuries earlier. That several merchants were able to make large donations leads us to infer that they were earning high profits from trade and also that they were trading on a much larger scale than the other merchants. Class differentiation was taking place in the merchant community separating the small trader from the large merchant.

The inscriptions are also replete with references to itinerant merchants who made donations to temples in towns which were far from their homes. This indicates a high volume of overland trade which was being carried on by individual merchants. Many of these merchants were from different parts of the Tamil country, but a significant proportion of itinerant merchants came from *malaimandalam*, the western hills of Kerala, participating in inter-regional overland trade. The western region produced two important commodities, namely pepper and areca nut. Traders known as *kudirai chetti* from the west also came to sell horses which had evidently been imported from Arabia to the ports on the west coast.

There are also occasional references to merchants from other regions, like Kaivaranadu in Karnataka and even Kashmiradesam.[58]

What were the factors which impelled merchants to make donations to temples instead of ploughing their surplus resources back in their own business? This question can only be answered inferentially since the factors motivating the merchants are not explicit. The stated objective of any donation was to earn religious merit. But there was the unstated need for the merchants as a class to enjoy the goodwill of local society. Merchants earning large profits are universally looked upon with suspicion as profiteers. Merchants used the donations to negate any antagonism and ill-will, and to be well regarded by their community by showing empathy for social concerns. Acceptance by society was perceived as tangible returns on their donations. For non-local merchants, there was the additional need to establish their credentials and identity in an area where they had no roots. Donations gave them visibility and respectability in places which were far from their homes.

## Merchant guilds

Merchants involved in long-distance and overseas trade were organized in guilds which were active all over south India. The term guild is used in a generic sense. Unlike the European guilds, the south Indian guilds were not governed by charters, strict constitutions or rules. Nor was their membership restricted with stringent conditions. Their amorphous structure and the variety of names adopted by the guilds in referring to themselves give rise to problems in arriving at definitive conclusions about their organization and their functioning. *Manigramam* and the *Disai-ayirattu-ainnurruvar* or the Five Hundred of the Thousand Directions, generally referred to as the *Ainnurruvar*, Five Hundred in short, were the two guilds mentioned most frequently in the inscriptions.

The earliest references to the merchant guild known as Manigramam occurred in inscriptions of the ninth or early tenth century in Kerala, a reflection of the long-established trade relations between the west coast and West Asia.[59] The inscription at Takua Pa in Thailand which also dates to the ninth century shows that the Manigramam guild was also well entrenched in trade in South-East Asia. In the Tamil region, the Manigramam guild was associated primarily with the town of Kodumbalur which is in Pudukkottai district. The chiefs of Kodumbalur were closely associated with the centres of power in the Chola empire and were linked to the dynasty through marriage. Pudukkottai was on the main trade route from places to the north and north-west of Tamilakam to the ports in the south, and its strategic location provided the ideal base for guilds involved in overland trade.

The Manigramam is mentioned in inscriptions from towns across the region over 400 years from the early decades of the tenth century till 1300, once again pointing to the longevity of institutions in Tamilakam. In almost every case, the reference is to an individual merchant who was making a donation to the local temple. The only reference to the guild as a group comes from the famous Piranmalai inscription of Ramnad district dated 1300 when the Kodumbalur Manigramam is mentioned as one of the many constituents of the Five Hundred. Individual merchants who were members of the Kodumbalur Manigramam had made donations to temples in towns as far apart as Salem, Sivapuri in Ramnad district and Nattam in Madurai district between 1000 and 1200.[60] Clearly, these were merchants participating in overland trade and travelling across the region. In the other references, the merchants identified themselves as members of the local Manigramam, like Uraiyur and Tillaisthanam (Tiruchi and Tanjavur districts).[61] The references to localized Manigramams indicate that the guild was a flexible organization which allowed such local associations to emerge under the umbrella of the parent body. It is also instructional to note that all the references to local Manigramams occurred prior to 1000, whereas the Kodumbalur Manigramam was active till 1300.

What purpose did the smaller local associations of the guild serve? It probably gave the merchants of different towns an overarching identity since they were affiliated with a parent organization which was well known, which still leaves us to wonder how these associations functioned vis-à-vis the local assembly of the nagaram. After the tenth century, however, there are no other references to the participation of this guild in overseas trade, and it would seem safe to conclude that the Manigramam was operating only in long-distance, intra- as well as inter-regional trade, but no longer in overseas trade. It was certainly overshadowed by the Five Hundred, which emerged as the largest and most visible association of merchants.

## Ainnurruvar: The Five Hundred

The most active and dominant guild was the Five Hundred, first mentioned in two inscriptions of Aihole in Karnataka, dating to 800. In Tamilakam, the oldest reference to the guild was in 927 in Pudukkottai district, and an undated inscription of the tenth century from

Ramnad district.[62] The Pudukkottai inscription refers to the *disai-ayirattu-ainnurruvar*. While the 'thousand directions' was a metaphor for the extended trade of the guild in all directions, what was signified by the term Five Hundred is not clear. It was probably derived from the eulogy of the guild which always mentioned that they held the *pancasata virasasanam*, five hundred charters, and observed the dharma of traders. There are references to groups of merchants in the ninth century, two referring to a group of 1700, and a third to a merchant group called the thousand of seven directions.[63] Were these precursors of the Five Hundred? The coincidence of the groups referring to themselves in numerical terms is intriguing.

Aihole was considered the original base for the Five Hundred of Tamilakam. Even Tamil inscriptions of the guild begin with a eulogy which claimed that the members were the children of the gods, Vasudeva, Kandali and Mulabhadra and of goddess Paramesvari of Ayyapolil or Ayyavole, both Tamil terms for Aihole. So, the guild seems to acknowledge that their organization originated in Aihole. Yet this association has been questioned. The first two Aihole inscriptions in fact referred to Brahmins learned in the Vedas and not to merchants. Later, almost the entire corpus of inscriptions on the Five Hundred in the tenth century was from

Tamilakam. The number of inscriptions from Karnataka began to increase in the eleventh century, though in the early decades of the century there were only three inscriptions which were all located in Mysore, then a part of the Chola empire.[64] The Chola campaign to conquer Mysore is itself attributed to the perceived need for controlling the main trade route from Tamilakam to the north and west and facilitating the movement of the Five Hundred.[65] The Five Hundred were active throughout south India and as well as in Sri Lanka, as is indicated by the distribution of the inscriptions. However, they were most active especially after 1100 in Karnataka and in Tamilakam. The highest number of inscriptions in Tamilakam is forty-six dated in the thirteenth century, followed by twenty-four in the tenth century. The Five Hundred remained very active between the tenth and the thirteenth centuries but began to slow down after 1300.[66]

The Five Hundred referred to themselves by a variety of descriptive appellations. Most often the term used was *Nanadesi*. There also references to the *Padinen-vishayam/vishayattar*, of the eighteen regions, and *Padinen-bhumi*, of the eighteen countries; the exact reason for using these descriptive appellations is not clear, but evidently all these terms referred to the Five Hundred.[67]

Other guilds also operated in the region—the

Valanjiyar, Anjuvannam and Chitrameli Periyanadu. The last is considered to have been a guild dealing in agricultural commodities which used a staff and plough as its emblem. The Anjuvannam was a guild of foreign merchants who had moved from the west coast to other coastal areas of south India. The term originally referred to Jewish merchants, but was later used with reference to Arab Muslim traders.[68] The Anjuvannam joined with the Valanjiyar on one occasion, and with other foreign merchants on another, to gift taxes to local temples,[69] acts by which they would have gained acceptance in local society, which again offers an insight to the behaviour of foreign merchants in host countries. The Valanjiyar were also referred to as the *vira-valanjiyar* of southern Sri Lanka. The adjective 'vira' to describe them was probably in reference to the fact that they were armed merchants.[70] Since the Five Hundred were also operating in Sri Lanka, this would indicate that merchants travelled freely between the two countries. The Valanjiyar also acted in consonance with the Five Hundred.

Five early inscriptions of the tenth and eleventh centuries refer to individual merchant members of the Five Hundred. The earliest dates to 981 and is the record of the gift of land for a lamp by a merchant of Konerirajapuram (Tanjavur district) who was a member of the Five Hundred. A second from Vedaranyam (Tanjavur district) dated 1000, refers to a donation made by the Five Hundred for or on behalf of a merchant. Three other inscriptions refer to donations made under the protection of the Five Hundred.[71] It is interesting that four inscriptions are from Tanjavur district and the fifth from Tiruchi district. It has been observed that though Pudukkottai is repeatedly emphasized as the strategically located centre of guild activities, more inscriptions about the Five Hundred occur in the Chola heartland areas of Tanjavur and Tiruchi which were clearly the nodes of guild operations.[72]

Who were the members of the Five Hundred? In inscriptions, the list of members follows the eulogy of the guild in the same vein of stylized ritual. The merchants of the eighteen cities, thirty-two coastal towns and sixty-four villages (*gatikai tavalam*); chettis and *kavarai*, another caste of merchants; *kamundasvami*, the headman among landholders; persons in lesser occupations and shopkeepers were all members of the guild. By the thirteenth century, this list had become longer and more detailed. Based on the details listed in inscriptions the members have been classified into ten categories as groups of big merchants; landholders; groups of local merchants trading in specific commodities; merchant warriors; warriors who protected merchants; foreign merchants; shopkeepers; artisans and craftsmen; writers and messengers; servants.[73] Ninety-five different names are used for individual groups in these categories which give an idea of the complexities of deconstructing inscriptions.

The maximum number of references is to warrior groups (twenty-one) and warrior merchants (eighteen) who are described as *nammakkal*, our children, indicating their subordinate status and the need of merchants for armed protection. Long-distance trade was a high-risk activity in medieval times and it is evident that the state was unable to provide adequate security to merchants. The armies employed by merchants also led to several towns being given the status of *erivirapattinam*. Though this term has been understood in many ways,[74] the more recently discovered inscription of Samuddirapatti in Madurai district dated 1050 as well as the inscriptions from Sri Lanka strongly indicate that a town was given the title of erivirapattinam in honour of the armed warriors like the *virakkodiyar*, those of the brave flag, who had fought off enemies of the Five Hundred.[75] They were also given certain concessions and benefits. Nearly all the inscriptions referring to erivirapattinams are dated between 1050 and 1100. It is not clear why such armed activity is not reported at all after 1200. Was there no further need for such protection, or had the

Five Hundred become powerful enough to obviate the necessity for employing soldiers for protection?

As the thirteenth century progressed, the composition of the Five Hundred became increasingly broad-based. The famous Piranmalai (Ramnad district) inscription of 1300 which runs into several pages in print gives a comprehensive list of all groups which constituted the assembly of the 'Eighteen Regions or Padinenvishayam of the four directions'. These included several assemblies of the Five Hundred which were said to be 'renowned in all quarters', and the nagarattar of several towns, including the nagarattar of Kodumbalur Manigramam.[76] The latter would lead us to infer that the Kodumbalur Manigramam had become a local traders' association. Several groups of Five Hundred were also referred to in the inscription of Tirumalai (Ramnad district) dated 1233.[77] All decisions of the Five Hundred were noted to be derived consensually by all the members assembled together. The guild thus had evolved from an association of merchants into an overarching organization which was a loose federation of affiliated merchant groups of different localities and towns.[78]

As their organization and activities expanded, the Five Hundred validated themselves through their association with temples. According to the eulogies of their inscriptions, their objectives were *aram valara kali meliya*, to promote religion and weaken the ill effects of Kali, for which they undertook acts in consonance with their professional dharma; an alternative reading would be, charitable acts of the guild assembly. By the thirteenth century they had a proprietary interest in several temples which were under their protection.[79]

In order to honour these commitments and fulfil their obligations, the full assembly of the constituents of the Five Hundred would meet and assign the taxes on all traded commodities to the temples. Whereas donations were made by individuals, corporate groups and even the Five Hundred throughout the Chola period, there was a distinct change of direction in the late twelfth and thirteenth centuries when the Chola state was in decline. The assembly of the guild began to fix tolls and taxes on commodities imported into and exported from various towns as also on goods in transit. These inscriptions do not even mention the ruling king which would indicate the degree of autonomy that the guild enjoyed and the extent to which it was de-linked from the organs of the state. Apart from the political implications, the details of tax imposts give a very clear indication of the range of goods traded and the extent of commerce. The taxes were referred to as *magamai* or *maganmai* in the earlier centuries and as *pattana-pagudi* in the later years; the latter term may also mean, the share of the town.[80]

Goods were transported in head loads, small or large sacks and on carts and were taxed accordingly. Small and large boats were also used to carry goods. The transportation network thus comprised both roads and internal waterways. The Piranmalai inscription gives the longest and most comprehensive list of goods traded, and specifies the rates of tax on cart loads, sacks and head loads. The commodities mentioned in the inscription were agricultural and primary products: rice, paddy, various lentils, salt; commercial crops: castor, areca nuts, pepper, turmeric, dried ginger, onions, mustard, cumin, myrobalans (*kadukkai*, *nelli* and *tanri* in Tamil; *har, amla* and *bela* in Hindi), cotton and sesamum; manufactured goods: yarn, coarse cloth, fine textiles, silk cloth; forest and aromatic products: wax, honey, sandalwood, eaglewood, rosewater, camphor; animals: sheep, horses, elephants; iron. Many of these were essential commodities in everyday use and were probably traded in local markets and towns. But even utility products like salt and pepper were traded over long distances—salt from coastal areas to inland markets, while pepper was brought from Kerala into Tamilakam. From this list we can also discern the internal linkages of textile production: from raw cotton to yarn (usually spun by women) to cloth, which was woven by special castes of weavers, and finally the merchants who traded in textiles, both coarse and fine.

A variety of luxury, high-value commodities like musk, conch, ivory, gems, coral and pearls, and metals like copper and brass were also traded. At the macro level, all this points to a great expansion in trade over the centuries in inland, inter-regional as well as overseas trade. The expansion of overseas trade is also corroborated by the findings of Chinese ceramic potsherds in ports on the east coast, which show a steady and growing volume of trade from the ninth century onward.[81]

## CONCLUSION

The synergy provided by the temple in the medieval period was critical in the development of trade and merchant associations. Individual merchants and larger groups found in the temple a larger identity and a public cause which integrated them with society and created acceptance for their trading activity. But questions can also be posed as to the other roles of corporate associations of merchants like nagaram and guilds. Since the intervention of the larger group was often sought when individual merchants either borrowed from the temple or promised to make a donation, it seems reasonable to conclude that the former, in fact, were not merely the guarantors of the transaction, but also would mediate in case of disputes. The nagaram or local assembly thus would deal with contractual obligations among local merchants, while the guild could intervene in disputes involving itinerant member merchants.

The expansion of trade in the thirteenth century when the Chola state was in decline is counter-intuitive since political stability and a strong state are considered necessary prerequisites for economic and commercial prosperity. In general, the tendency to over-tax and victimize merchants was strong in times of political instability; but it was also recognized that this was self-defeating in the long run. Thus, rulers, even lesser chiefs, remained committed to promoting trade. In this context, the declaration made by the chief of Motupalli in Bapatla, Guntur district, in 1358 is particularly illuminating. He offered full freedom in his town to merchants and nanadesis to travel and to sell their goods as they pleased; duties on gold, silver and exported sandalwood and other taxes were reduced. Finally, the town was declared to be a sanctuary.[82]

The strengthening of merchant groups through institutional structures like the guilds and assemblies was clearly able to counteract the political negative of a weakening state and the Motupalli inscription also indicates that the guild had the power to exert pressure on local rulers to prevent undue exactions on merchants and trade. The guilds also derived their strength from their consistent interaction with temples as a reference point which fortified their position. It was this strong base that ensured the continued survival, viability and stability of the economy and trade independent of political conditions.

# 5. THE TAMIL MERCHANT
# DOWN THE AGES:
# A RETROSPECT

THE THOUSAND YEARS from the age of Sangam
literature to the end of the Chola Empire was truly the
millennium of the Tamil merchants. The resilience of
the Tamil merchants, mercantile institutions and trade
over more than a thousand years, notwithstanding social
and political change within the region and in the larger
world of maritime commerce, can be attributed to several
factors. The Tamil region had extensive trade links even
prior to its recorded history. The internal economy of
Tamilakam had a strong link with overseas markets, and
the region enjoyed a favourable trade balance from its
external trade. This advantage was clearly derived from
the high level of demand in markets around the world
for the textiles produced in Tamilakam and in India as a
whole, as well as for commodities like pepper. In turn,

many commodities were also imported into Tamilakam, ranging from tin, lead and copper used in coinage and metal work and horses to high-value products like coral and aromatic substances. Without such a range of imports, the imports which comprised a high share of precious metals would have resulted in inflationary pressures and destabilized the economy.

The economy was also not excessively or exclusively oriented to overseas trade. The export trade was grounded in a large volume of internal trade within the region, as well as overland and coastal trade with other parts of India. The economy thus had the stability of an adequate level of effective domestic demand which was a prerequisite for long-term economic viability.

The growth of trade was built on urbanization and growth of cities. In the Sangam age, urbanization was restricted to ports and inland capitals. Nevertheless, these were vibrant centres of economic activity, bustling with traders, shops and bazaars functioning throughout the day and late into the night. Many levels of trading were carried on in cities. Most local traders were actually vendors selling their wares on the streets. But shops existed at a higher level of retail activity involving greater capital. Overseas trade called for large amounts of investments and reserves of capital, not only because the goods traded tended to be high-value goods but also since each merchant would be dealing in large import or export shipments. These merchants should correctly be regarded as the merchant capitalists of their day. The pace of urbanization increased during the medieval period reflecting the expansion of economic activity and trade, as well as the development of merchant institutions.

The consolidation of political authority under the Tamil kingdoms created a qualitatively different environment in several ways. During the ancient period, Tamil polity was fragmented and the region was ruled by many small chieftains and war lords. Trade continued with little disruption not because general peace and order prevailed in Tamilakam, but because, despite frequent wars and conflicts, the rulers did not impede trade with extortionate demands and oppression. Foreign traders were allowed to come and trade in peace and they often stayed for long periods in the ports and also in inland cities without hindrance.

During the medieval period, the situation changed because the political environment stabilized after the emergence of strong kingdoms in Tamilakam, first under the Pallavas and Pandyas, and later especially under the Cholas. The two most distinctive institutions of Tamil polity that came to the fore during this period were the corporate assemblies of the villages and towns and the regional assembly with their broad-based membership and democratic functioning; and the temple.

Both institutions have excited the interest of historians. The village assemblies, in fact, offer a model for decentralized administration which would be relevant even today for any state interested in promoting local government. But it was the nagaram, the assembly of the town and merchants, which was important for trade. It must be remembered that in the predominantly agricultural economy of the times, neither the nagaram as an institution nor merchants as individuals were completely dissociated from land ownership or management. Society was thus characterized not by sharp polarization but by integration.

The temple developed as a dominant and integrative institution during this period. It was a major player in the economy in its own right. More importantly, it became a depository institution which attracted donations of gold, money, land and livestock as well as deposits of money. Both were circulated in the local economy on well-specified terms of interest to be paid in kind to maintain temple services, and in the process the temple became the medium for redistributing the surplus which came under its control. By participating in donations and temple management, merchants and the larger associations of nagaram and guild earned social acceptance and recognition.

While nagarams were concerned with local trade, guilds like the Five Hundred were important in itinerant trade because they offered more security to their members. Trading in the pre-medieval and medieval period was predicated on minimizing risk—the risks of unknown market conditions and the physical risks of itinerant trade. This was solved through forming collective associations which offered security to members, and the long-term viability of the associations is clearly evident from their continued strength even after the decline of the Chola Empire. Guilds were especially visible in overseas markets in South-East Asia and Sri Lanka. All itinerant trade involved physical danger and risk, and guilds employed armed warriors to protect their interests. However, collective institutions accommodated the independence of individual merchants, and there is little evidence that guild members traded as a group; the advantage of guild membership was that it served to provide a larger identity and implicit security to member merchants.

The Chola state pursued an aggressive military policy of conquest which also served to promote mercantile interests. Even though its primary motivation was imperial expansion, the enlarged Chola state offered greater opportunities to merchant groups to penetrate into other regions and overseas markets. Further, the treasure captured during military expeditions found its way to temples in the form of donations which were circulated in the local economy.

Last, and perhaps most important, merchants were generally well regarded in Tamil society. The degree of social acceptance was an important psychological factor which helped the merchants to function in strength. Merchants had earned the acceptance and good will of society especially through their interaction with the temple. Society was not characterized by binary division between landed interests and merchants, and social integration enabled trade to function in a favourable climate.

While the rise of strong kingdoms and a centralized state helped the growth of trade, the decline of the kingdoms did not automatically lead to major disruptions to trade. When the state was powerful, it gave active support to merchants. But even in times of political instability, trade continued to grow—as happened in Tamilakam throughout the thirteenth century. This was in part due to the fact that lesser chiefs understood that their interests would be better served in the long run when merchants were not victimized and trade could be carried on without undue demands or pressures. The development of strong corporate institutions which could function with great autonomy irrespective of the state ensured that merchants could continue to trade without serious disruptions. In the final analysis, the social, political and institutional environment was more crucial for the perpetuation of trade and business in the medieval period than any strategy of business as such.

This account of the merchants still leaves many questions unanswered. How did merchants participate in maritime trade? Did they own ships or did they carry their goods on ships owned by others? Alternatively, did they send their cargo as consignments with the vessel owners to be sold in overseas markets either through their own correspondent merchants or by the ship's captain? We cannot really answer these questions, nor can we answer questions about the functioning of capital and credit markets and related business practices. The data constraints are many since the inscriptions provide only scattered and ambiguous information which has to be collated very carefully to provide meaningful insights and analysis. There are no extant literary sources for the medieval period to supplement the inscriptions, and personal documents or papers of merchants are non-existent. In spite of these drawbacks, we are still able to derive an overall picture which leaves us wondering at the highly sophisticated economic and social institutions that evolved in the pre-modern period, and the long-term survival of trade and mercantile operation.

# APPENDIX

## A NOTE ON TAMIL SOURCES

TWO KINDS OF sources are used for studying the history of the Tamil region in the pre-modern period: literary works and inscriptions. For the ancient period, generally referred to as the Sangam age dating to the first to the fourth century CE, the corpus of literary works of the period is the primary source used for historical reconstruction. Mainly, the works comprise eight anthologies of poetry, of which the best known are probably *Ahananuru* and *Purananuru*, the two collections of 400 poems each. These are the 400 of the inner world and the 400 of the external world, the former dealing with the theme of love and the latter with the theme of war. Selections from these poems have been translated by A.K. Ramanujan. However, these offer little scope for purposes of economic history, though there are a few infrequent references to ports and trade. The ninth group of poems is a collection of ten poems, known as *Pattupattu*. The poems are of varying lengths, ranging from 103 to 782 lines. The longest poem is

*Maduraikkanchi*, which describes the rule of the Pandya king and his capital, Madurai. With one or two exceptions, these poems give a detailed account of trade, ports, shipping, merchants and urban life, which are highly evocative and recreate the ancient world in visually vivid descriptions.

To these we must add the two major epics, *Silappadikaram* and *Manimekalai* generally ascribed to the fifth century CE, with strong overtones of Jain and Buddhist influence. Tiruvalluvar, the author of the great Tamil work on ethics, *Tirukkural*, is also generally believed to have been a Jain. The last, unfortunately, is of little interest to the economic historian, unlike the *Arthasastra*. But the *Silappadikaram* and *Manimekalai* are generally taken with the Sangam poems as sources of history because their stories relate to the Sangam age. Many Tamil scholars in fact believe that they were written during the first or second century CE, placing them in the Sangam age.

It must be clarified that none of these works were 'lost' in any sense and rediscovered in the modern era. Medieval commentators like Adiyarkkunallar and Parimelalagar had written commentaries on the *Silappadikaram* and *Tirukkural* respectively in the thirteenth century or so, while another commentator, Nachchinarkkiniyar, who had done the commentary on the *Pattupattu*, probably belonged to a somewhat later date. The Sangam poems, the epics, the *Tirukkural* and other works were known to the limited world of Tamil scholars and existed only in palm leaf manuscripts. The credit for bringing these works into the public arena should go to U.V. Swaminatha Aiyar (referred to as the grandfather of Tamil) who began to publish these works, along with the original commentary and additional notes. The first edition of the *Silappadikaram* was published by him in 1892, though there were two earlier prints of only the first canto which had come out in 1872 and 1880. These works have been reprinted frequently since then, and many translations are also available.

It is very difficult for the lay reader to understand the language and style of Tamil of the Sangam works. Fortunately, student editions are available which give a word for word 'translation' of the original into modern Tamil, which makes it much easier for non-specialist readers.

Temple inscriptions constitute the main source of information for the medieval period. The social custom of inscribing every kind of local transaction or occurrence on the walls of local temples is a boon for historians. Thousands of inscriptions have been published in the series of *South Indian Inscriptions* and *Epigraphia Indica*. In addition there are special volumes of inscriptions from the Tirupati temple and so on. The serious student of history would go to Mysore to the Epigraphy office, where many more thousands of inscriptions can be found which are yet to be printed.

Inscriptions usually start with a *meykirtti* or eulogy of the ruling king. It is from the eulogies that the dates of major historical events like wars and military campaigns have been reconstructed. For instance, the major conquests of Rajaraja I and the maritime invasion and conquest of Sri

Vijaya by Rajendra I are known only because of the eulogies of the inscriptions. Inscriptions also mention the regnal year of the king, and give the date according to the Tamil (Indian) calendar, mentioning the year in the sixty-year cycle, the month and day, the phase of the moon, the ascendant star of the day and other details. Based on an Indian ephemeris this information was correlated with the corresponding dates in the western calendar, which enabled the determination of the calendar coordinates for the history of medieval India.

One section from the epic *Manimekalai* is given below, with the Tamil original, to give the general reader an insight into the Tamil works.

## Crossing the streets (of Kanchipuram)

[Here was] the broad street on which the security guards of shops lived; streets housing people following many occupations [like]: fish mongers selling many varieties of fish; sellers of white salt; women selling toddy; traders selling varieties of sweets and cooked food; sellers of mutton; sellers of betel leaves; sellers of five varieties of aromatic substances; potters; copper and brass smiths who made metal pots; goldsmiths who fashioned articles of gold; carpenters working on wood; masons; painters who made pictures of gods; leather workers; tailors; makers of flower garlands; people who told time; musicians of great ability who sang on many themes; conch cutters who made bangles

# Manimekalai 28.4 lines 29–61

## *Kachchi Managar Pukka Kadai* (Entry into the great city of Kanchi)
## The streets of Kanchi

### 4. தெருக்களைக் கடந்தாள்

கடைகாப் பமைந்த காவ லாளர்
மிடைகொண் டியங்கும் வியன்மலி மறுகும்,                30
பன்மீன் விலைலஞர், வெள்ளுப்புப் பகருநர்,
கண்ணெணடை யாட்டியர், காழியர், கூவியர்,
மைந்நிண விலைலஞர், பாசவர், வாசவர்
என்னுநர் மறுகும்; இருங்கோ வேட்கரும்,
செம்பு செய்ஞ்ஞேரும்; கஞ்ச காரரும்                    35
பைம்பொன் செய்ஞ்ஞேரும், பொன்செய் கொல்லரும்,
மரங்கொல் தச்சரும், மண்ணீட் டாளரும்,
வரந்தர வெழுதிய ஓவிய மாக்களும்

தோலின் துன்னரும், துன்ன வினைஞரும்,
மாலைக் காரரும், காலக் கணிதரும்,                     40
நலந்தரு பண்ணும் திறனும் வாய்ப்ப;
நிலங்கலங் கண்டம் நிகழுக் காட்டும்
பாணர், என்றிவர் பல்வகை மறுகும்;
விலங்கரம் பொருளுடம் வெள்வளை போஞ்நரோடு
இலங்குமணி வினைஞர் இரீஇய பறுகும்;                   45
வேத்தியல் பொதுவியல் என்றிவ் விரண்டின்
கூத்தியல்பு அறிந்த கூத்தியர் மறுகும்;
பால்வே ராக எண்வகைப் பட்ட
கூலங் குலைஇய கூல மறுகும்,
மாகதர், சூதர்வே தாளிகர் மறுகும்;                    50
போகம் புரக்கும் பொதுவர்பொலி மறுகும்;
கண்ணுழை கல்லா நுண்ணூற் கைவினை
வண்ண அறுவையர் வளந்திகழ் மறுகும்;
பொன்னுரை காண்போர் நன்மனை மறுகும்;
பன்மணி பகர்வோர் மன்னிய மறுகும்;                    55

மறையோர் அருந்தொழில் குறையா மறுகும்;
அரைசியல் மறுகும்; அமைச்சியல் மறுகும்
எனைப்பெருஞ் தொழில்செய் ஏனோர் மறுகும்;
மன்றமும், பொதியிலும், சந்தியும், சதுக்கமும்,
புதுக்கோள் யானையும் பொற்றார்ப் புரவியும்,              60
கதிக்குற வடிப்போர் கவின்பெறு வீதியும்;

of white conch; jewellers who made ornaments with *navaratna*, glowing gems; well-trained men and women street performers.

Then there was the street of grain merchants where the eight varieties of grain were stacked in separate heaps; the street of minstrels and bards and town criers who announced the time; the street where courtesans who gave sexual pleasure lived; the prosperous area where skilled weavers lived, who produced cloths so fine that the eye could not discern the yarn in the weave.

Streets with the beautiful houses of assayers of gold; streets where many gem sellers lived; where the Brahmins lived; the main royal street; the street where ministers and important state officials lived; the public areas of the city assemblies, and squares and street corners.

Streets where trainers for the elephants which had just been brought into the city and for horses wearing golden chains lived. [Manimekalai walked along all these streets looking around.]

# NOTES

## Prologue: A Historical Background

1. This section draws on standard histories of India, and especially Nilakanta Sastri, *A History of South India*.

2. Authorities like U.V. Swaminatha Aiyar and many other Tamil scholars, however, believe that the two were written during the Sangam period, and date to the first or second century.

## 1. Merchants and Trade in the Pre-modern Era

1. Curtin, *Cross-Cultural Trade*, 11, 38.

2. J.C. van Leur in his seminal work, *Indonesian Trade and Society*, had concluded that pre-modern Asian trade was primarily 'peddling' trade of high value goods, 'splendid but trifling'.

3. Sangam literature refers to the body of poems which were produced by many individual poets till the fourth century of the Common Era. I have particularly drawn on the long poems which are referred to collectively as

*Pattupattu* (The Ten Songs). The Sangam was a literary conclave based in the Pandyan capital of Madurai. The only extant literature of this genre is from the last Sangam. This material is used along with the two Tamil epics *Silappadikaram* and *Manimekalai*, which many Tamil scholars believe belong to the first or second century CE. The more accepted school of thought among historians is that the epics belong to the fifth or sixth century CE.

## 2. Trade and Merchants in Ancient Tamilakam

1. *Silappadikaram*, I.viii.1–4.
2. Earlier historians like Kanakasabhai were not clear about the exact location of Vanji. However, all later historians have definitively identified Vanji with the modern town of Karur.
3. Mahadevan, *Early Tamil Epigraphy*, 43–46.
4. Nilakanta Sastri, *South India*, 139.
5. Champakalakshmi calls them 'chiefdoms' and urges that the interpretation of *vendar* as kings should be reconsidered. ('Urbanisation in Medieval Tamil Nadu', 36–37.)
6. *Maduraikkanchi* (one of the ten *Pattuppattu*) is about Neduncheliyan's exploits; *Pattinappalai* (also of the *Pattuppattu*) is about Tirumavalavan; *Silappadikaram*, III is an account of the Chera king; and *Perumpanarruppadai* (from the *Pattuppattu*) is about Ilantiraiyan.

7. Raghava Aiyengar, 'Ancient Dravidian Industries', 78–79.

8. *Maduraikkanchi*, 120–22.

9. Mukund, *Trading World*, 14–15.

10. *Ahananuru* and *Purananuru* 56, quoted by Raghava Aiyengar, 'Ancient Dravidian Industries', 85.

11. The location of many ports has been identified on the basis of the map in Kanakasabhai, *Tamils*, 23.

12. *Sirupanarruppadai*, 62.

13. *Maduraikkanchi*, 78–88.

14. Ibid. 316–26.

15. Mahadevan, *Early Tamil Epigraphy*, Map 1, 34; 153.

16. *Silappadikaram*, II.xiv.106–110.

17. The term used in the poem is 'Kalagam', which is also taken to mean Burma. Kadaram, the Tamil name for Kedah in Malaysia, is the preferred reading. The reference to gold also supports this reading, for this region was also known as Suvarnadvipa or island of gold.

18. *Pattinappalai*, 184–93; 29–31; 172–73.

19. *Silappadikaram*, I.ii.5–7; I.vi.152–55.

20. *Sirupanarruppadai*, 152, 155.

21. *Perumpanarruppadai*, 319–24.

22. *Periplus*, 46.

23. Schoff, 'Introduction', *Periplus*, 4–6.

24. Nilakanta Sastri, *Foreign Notices*, 5–6.

25. Quoted by Kanakasabhai, *Tamils*, 32.

26. Suresh, *Symbols of Trade*, 30–31.

27. Ibid. 29–30; Mahadevan, *Early Tamil Epigraphy*, 43–44.

28. Quoted in Kanakasabhai, *Tamils*, 32–33; Nilakanta Sastri, *Foreign Notices*, 52–53.

29. Iron and high-quality steel were exported from India for many centuries, down to the eighteenth century.

30. Suresh, *Symbols of Trade*, 31–32; Mahadevan, *Early Tamil Epigraphy*, 44, 153.

31. Nilakanta Sastri, *Foreign Notices*, 7–8.

32. *Periplus*, 44–45. The ports have been identified based on Nilakanta Sastri, *Foreign Notices*, 57.

33. *Periplus*, 44–45.

34. Schoff, Notes to the *Periplus*, 227.

35. Quoted by Mahadevan, *Early Tamil Epigraphy*, 155.

36. Quoted by Champakalakshmi, *Trade, Ideology, Urbanization*, 121.

37. *Purananuru* 343, quoted by Kanakasabhai, *Tamils*, 16.

38. *Periplus*, 46.

39. Mahadevan, *Early Tamil Epigraphy*, 155–56.

40. Suresh, *Symbols of Trade*, 156.

41. Ibid. 33–34.

42. Ibid. 155.

43. Nilakanta Sastri, *Foreign Notices*, 4–5, 44–45; 10.

44. Rajan Gurukkal, cited in Mukund, *Trading World*, 19.

45. Mahadevan, *Early Tamil Epigraphy*, 153.

46. Suresh, *Symbols of Trade*, 47–51; 52–65.

47. Raghava Aiyengar, 'Ancient Dravidian Industries', 81.

48. *Maduraikkanchi*, 513; *Silappadikaram*, II.xiv.205–207.

49. *Silappadikaram*, I.v.15–16.

50. *Maduraikkanchi*, 433, 554; *Perumpanarruppadai*, 469–70; *Sirupanarruppadai*, 235–36; *Porunarruppadai*, 82–83; *Malaipadukadam*, 561.

51. *Manimekalai*, xix.107–109.

52. *Silappadikaram*, II.xiv.168–79.

53. *Maduraikkanchi*, 766–70; 152–58.

54. *Perumpanarruppadai*, 39–41; 81–82.

55. Ibid. 81.

56. *Pattinappalai*, 118–25, 133–39.

57. *Silappadikaram*, I.v.110–17.

58. *Silappadikaram*, I.vi.144.

59. Curtin, *Cross-Cultural Trade*, 6, 75.

60. *Pattinappalai*, 206–25.

61. *Maduraikkanchi*, 500.

62. *Perumpanarruppadai*, 66–67.

63. *Manimekalai*, xxii, 111–14; *Silappadikaram*, II.xv.163.

64. *Perumpanarruppadai*, 68–75.

65. *Silappadikaram*, I.i.23–25; 30–35.

66. *Silappadikaram*, I.ii.8–9.

67. Mahadevan, *Early Tamil Epigraphy*, nos. 39, 42, 43, 46, 69 and 70.

68. *Silappadikaram*, I.v.1–2; 41–42; I.vi.120–122; *Maduraikkanchi*, 500–502; *Pattinappalai*, 140–47.

69. Raghava Aiyengar, 'Ancient Dravidian Industries', 97.

70. In fact, the name is derived from the word *kir* which denotes cutting, as well as the harsh sound made during the process of cutting conchs.

71. Raghava Aiyengar, 'Ancient Dravidian Industries', 90.

72. *Silappadikaram*, I.ii.5–7.

73. Rajan Gurukkal, cited in Mukund, *Trading World*, 14.

74. Champakalakshmi and Moti Chandra, cited in Mukund, *Trading World*, 18.

75. Mahadevan, *Early Tamil Epigraphy*, 141; nos 3, 6.

76. Ibid. 141.

77. *Silappadikaram*, II.xiv.180–200. This very long passage has been abridged for easier reading.

78. Ibid. 201–204.

79. Ibid. 205–208.

80. *Maduraikkanchi*, 366–67; *Pattinappalai*, 179–83; *Perumpanarruppadai*, 336–37.

81. *Sirupanarruppadai*, 54–61.

82. *Perumpanarruppadai*, 46–65. This translation omits the many poetic metaphors of the original.

83. According to the dictionary, the term *umanar* referred to salt merchants as well as manufacturers of salt.

84. *Perumpanarruppadai*, 77–80.

85. Ibid. 39–41, 80–82. See also, note 10, above.

86. *Silappadikaram*, I.v.38, 50.

87. *Silappadikaram*, II.xiv.209–210.

88. *Silappadikaram*, I.v.9–12.

89. *Silappadikaram*, I.vi.130–31.

90. *Silappadikaram*, I.v.110–114.

91. *Maduraikkanchi*, 315–16.

92. Champakalakshmi, *Trade, Ideology, Urbanization*, 109.

93. *Silappadikaram*, II.xiv.66–67.

94. *Mullaippattu*, 65–66.

95. *Mullaippattu*, 61; *Nedunalvadai*, 101.

96. *Manimekalai*, xix.106.

97. *Silappadikaram*, III.xxx.160. Scholars like U.V. Swaminatha Iyer have dated the epic to the second century CE based on this internal evidence.

98. Karashima, 'Tamil Inscriptions', in Karashima, *Ancient and Medieval Commercial Activities in the Indian Ocean*, 10.

99. Maloney, 'Archaeology in South India', *Essays on South India*, 12.

100. *Silappadikaram*, I.v.13–39.

101. Ibid. 40–55.

102. Ibid. 59–64.

103. *Silappadikaram*, I.vi.134–51.

104. *Silappadikaram*, I.v.157; *Manimekalai*, I.17.

105. Mahadevan, *Early Tamil Epigraphy*, 125.

106. *Silappadikaram*, II.xxi.39, 57; III.xxiv.24.

107. *Silappadikaram*, II.xiv.62–69.

108. *Maduraikkanchi*, 424–28; 694–99.

109. *Maduraikkanchi*, 360; 429–30; 536–44.

110. *Silappadikaram*, I.v.169–73; II.xiv.6–13; *Maduraikkanchi*, 466–70, 476–80.

111. Champakalakshmi, *Trade, Ideology, Urbanization*, 94–95.

## 3. State, Polity and Overseas Relations under the Tamil Kingdoms

1. Nilakanta Sastri called this period 'a long historical night'. *South India*, 144.

2. Minakshi, *Pallavas*, 15, f.n.

3. Tirumangai Alvar, *Periya Tirumoli*, II.3.9 and 10.

4. Ibid. II.9.1 to 9.

5. Ibid. II.6.6.

6. Nilakanta Sastri, *Foreign Notices*, 116–17.

7. Minakshi, *Pallavas*, 25; Nilakanta Sastri, *South India*, 154.

8. The complexity of local administration, especially under the Cholas, has been studied extensively. This section draws on Nilakanta Sastri, *Colas*, ch. 18; Minakshi, *Pallavas*, 141–50; Hall, *Trade and Statecraft*, ch. 2.

9. Interestingly, the Chettiyars, the major trading caste in Tamil Nadu, still refer to themselves as 'nagarattar'. In fact, they claim that all historical references to the nagarattar are about their community. In truth, however, in the pre-modern period, the term is used only in the non-specific, general sense of a member of the nagaram assembly, or a merchant.

10. The location of inscriptions in *South Indian Inscriptions* (hereafter *SII*) and other published volumes is given with reference to districts as mentioned in *SII*, and as they used to be, even though at present the villages or towns might be located in the newly formed districts after the extensive reorganization of district administration in the post-Independence period, when larger districts were split into many smaller districts.

11. *SII*, 22.1, 77 and 80.

12. This section is based primarily on Shanmugam, *Revenue*

*System*; Nilakanta Sastri, *Colas*, ch. 19 and Hall, *Trade and Statecraft*, ch. 4 have also been referred to.

13. Karashima, *History and Society*, ch. 1.

14. Shanmugam, *Revenue System*, 80–88; Nilakanta Sastri, *Colas*, 528–29.

15. Shanmugam, *Revenue System*, 237–40 has a full list of inscriptions mentioning revenue surveys.

16. Nilakanta Sastri, *Colas*, 536–39.

17. Society in south India was divided vertically into two groups referred to as right- and left-hand castes. Each group combined several castes, which acted as a homogeneous, unified interest group because of the overarching identity of the caste grouping. This social phenomenon which disappeared during the nineteenth century has excited much attention among historians. For a brief account and additional references, see Mukund, *Trading World*, 145–50.

18. *SII*, 5, 976, dated 1065, Tiruvenkadu in Tanjavur district.

19. *SII*, 7, 107, 13th century, Tiruvottur in North Arcot district.

20. Hall, *Trade and Statecraft*, 58.

21. *SII*, 12, 224, Tiruvalanchuli, Tanjavur.

22. *SII*, 7, 1000.

23. *SII*, 8, 303.

24. *SII*, 22, 360.

25. Shanmugam, *Revenue System*, 141–43.

26. For a brief history of the South-East Asian kingdoms from the fourth century till the thirteenth century, see

---

Majumdar, *History and Culture of the Indian People*, Vol. 3, ch. 24; Vol. 4, ch. 14; Vol. 5, ch. 21.

27. Nilakanta Sastri, *South India*, 203.

28. For an analysis of the inscriptions and the texts, see K.V. Ramesh 'Cultural Intercourse between India and South-east Asia' and 'Texts of Inscriptions' in Karashima, *Commercial Activities in the Indian Ocean*, 147–59; 209–26.

29. For the texts and analyses of the inscriptions, see Karashima, 'Tamil Inscriptions', 10–18; Subbarayalu, 'Inscription at Barus', 19–26; both in Karashima, *Ancient and Medieval Commercial Activities in the Indian Ocean*.

30. Nilakanta Sastri, *Foreign Notices*, 45.

31. Ibid. 83.

32. Ibid. 116–17.

33. Ibid. 145, fn 25.

34. Majumdar, *History and Culture of the Indian People*, Vol. 4, 444–46; Nilakanta Sastri, *Colas*, 219, 316.

35. Hall, *Trade and Statecraft*, 175.

36. Karashima, 'Tamil Inscriptions', in Karashima, *Ancient and Medieval Commercial Activities in the Indian Ocean*, 15–16.

37. Majumdar, *History and Culture of the Indian People*, Vol. 5, 730–32; Nilakanta Sastri, *South India*, 182, 183–84.

38. Nilakanta Sastri, *Colas*, 219.

39. Ibid. 211–21.

40. Ibid. 318–19.

41. Minakshi, *Pallavas*, 15, 20; Nilakanta Sastri, *South India*, ch. 8.
42. Nilakanta Sastri, *Colas*, 121–24.
43. Ibid. 172–73.
44. For a comprehensive account, Ibid. 248–53.
45. Ibid. 316–19.
46. Spencer, 'Temple Money-lending', 291–92.
47. The Tamil inscriptions of the Nanadesi merchant guild in Sri Lanka have been analysed in detail by S. Pathmanathan, 'Lankatilaka Temple Inscriptions', 'Nanadesis in Anuradhapura' and 'Trade and Urbanisation in Medieval Sri Lanka', 36–47; 48–56; 62–71; and, Karashima and Subbarayalu, 'Inscription from Viharehinna' and 'Ainnurruvar', 27–39; 72–88; in Karashima, *Ancient and Medieval Commercial Activities in the Indian Ocean*.

## 4. The Temple, Nagaram and Merchants

1. Nilakanta Sastri, *South India*, 461–71.
2. Champakalakshmi, 'Urbanisation in Medieval Tamil Nadu', 38–39.
3. *SII*, 13, 251.
4. *SII*, 7, 118.
5. The subsequent sections of this chapter are based extensively on inscriptions published in *SII*. Individual inscriptions are cited only when relevant.
6. *SII*, 2.2, 24.

7. Appadorai, *Economic Conditions*, 1, 274–300.

8. Stein, 'A Medieval South Indian Temple', 68–82.

9. *SII*, 4, 511; also, *SII*, 24, 167.

10. Nilakanta Sastri, *Colas*, 580–81; Tirumalai, *Land Grants and Agrarian Reactions*, 6–7.

11. *SII*, 17, 326.

12. *SII*, 7, 785; *SII*, 22.1, 41.

13. These numbers however varied from 90 to 96 sheep. Sometimes even as few as two cows were donated.

14. It is difficult to convert volumetric units of alakku, ulakku, uri etc. into measurement units used today. Two ulakkus made one uri, and was probably equivalent to about 500 ml.

15. Spencer, 'Temple Money-lending', 281–82.

16. *SII*, 3.1, 18; *SII*, 7, 870, both dating to the early 11th century CE.

17. See *SII*, 12, which has inscriptions of the Pallava period.

18. *SII*, 12, 34.

19. *SII*, 3.3, 105.

20. *SII*, 17, 235 from Melsevur, South Arcot.

21. Shanmugam, *Revenue System*, 263.

22. Spencer, 'Temple Money-lending', 277–93.

23. Mukund, *Trading World*, 32–34.

24. Hall, *Trade and Statecraft*, 57–58.

25. Champakalakshmi, 'Urbanisation in Medieval Tamil Nadu'.

26. *SII*, 26, 103.

27. *SII*, 7, 1005.

28. SII, 12, 34.

29. Hall, *Trade and Statecraft*, ch. 5.

30. Champakalakshmi, 'Urbanisation in Medieval Tamil Nadu', 46.

31. *SII*, 2.2, 37.

32. *SII*, 17, 326.

33. Hall, *Trade and Statecraft*, 125–26.

34. *SII*, 4, 223.

35. Hall, *Trade and Statecraft*, 55–56.

36. *SII*, 23, 262, dated 924–25.

37. *SII*, 26, 276, dated 1171.

38. Champakalakshmi, 'Urbanisation in Medieval Tamil Nadu', 49–50.

39. *SII*, 7, 901; *SII*, 22.1, 41; *SII*, 26, 401.

40. *SII*, 22.2, 442.

41. See, for instance, the list of streets in Tanjavur. *SII*, 2.3, 94, 95.

42. *SII*, 3.3, 125.

43. Hall, *Trade and Statecraft*, 80–81.

44. *SII*, 13,133; *SII*, 23, 254.

45. *SII*, 23, 212.

46. *SII*, 13, 214.

47. *SII*, 5, 492.

48. *SII*, 22.2, 442.

49. *SII*, 6, 40, 41; *SII*, 26, 11.

50. *SII*, 17, 679.

51. *SII*, 17, 331.

52. *SII*, 17, 310 and 326.

53. Mukund, *Trading World*, 33–34.
54. *SII*, 19, 400.
55. *SII*, 4, 512; also *SII*, 24, 168. The amount stated is very large; one can only surmise that land prices in Srirangam were very high.
56. *SII*, 8, 294; *SII*, 17, 461.
57. *SII*, 17, 455.
58. *SII*, 24, 127; *SII*, 14, 197.
59. Abraham, *Two Merchant Guilds*, ch. 1.
60. *SII*, 4, 147; *SII*, 14, 235; *Avanam* 3.15.3, 37.
61. *SII*, 5, 590, Tillaisthanam, dated 934; *SII*, 13, 26, Srinivasanallur, dated 1000 CE; *SII*, 13, 28, Tiruvellarai, dated 1000 CE.
62. 'Texts of Select Inscriptions', Appendix 2 in Karashima, *Commercial Activities in the Indian Ocean*, 228–29.
63. *SII*, 14, 9 and 16; *Avanam* 11.7.6, 21.
64. Karashima, 'South Indian and Sri Lankan Inscriptions' in Karashima, *Commercial Activities in the Indian Ocean*, 3–9.
65. Champakalakshmi, 'Urbanisation in Medieval Tamil Nadu', 55.
66. Karashima, 'South Indian and Sri Lankan Inscriptions' in Karashima, *Commercial Activities in the Indian Ocean*, 5–6.
67. Karashima, 'South Indian and Sri Lankan Inscriptions' in Karashima, *Commercial Activities in the Indian Ocean*, 4.
68. Champakalakshmi, 'Urbanisation in Medieval Tamil Nadu', 36; 'South Indian Guilds' in *Trade, Ideology,*

*Urbanization*, 312–13. Champakalakshmi, in fact, identifies the Padinen vishayam with the Chitrameli Periyanadu. She is also of the view that the name Anjuvannam is derived from the word Anjuman, which means assembly.

69. Inscriptions dated 1269 at Tittandatanapuram, Ramnad and 1279 at Kistnapatam (Nellore district, AP). Reproduced in Karashima, *Commercial Activities in the Indian Ocean*, 270, 274.

70. *SII*, 6, 20; *SII*, 19, 459.

71. *SII*, 19, 280; 216; 4 and 170. *SII*, 23, 143.

72. Karashima, 'South Indian and Sri Lankan Inscriptions' in Karashima, *Commercial Activities in the Indian Ocean*, 5–6.

73. Karashima and Subbarayalu, 'Ainnurruvar' in Karashima, *Commercial Activities in the Indian Ocean*, 76–79. This is based on inscriptions in Tamil and Kannada.

74. Hall considered these towns to be higher order trading centres dealing with the nagaram, while Champakalakshmi took them to be protected warehouses of itinerant merchants. Hall, *Trade and Statecraft*, 173; Champakalakshmi, 'Urbanisation in Medieval Tamil Nadu', 52.

75. Karashima, 'South Indian and Sri Lankan Inscriptions' in Karashima, *Commercial Activities in the Indian Ocean*, 7–8.

76. *SII*, 8, 442.
77. Champakalakshmi, 'Urbanisation in Medieval Tamil Nadu', 31; 'South Indian Guilds' in *Trade, Ideology, Urbanization*, 315–16.
78. Karashima and Subbarayalu, 'Ainnurruvar' in Karashima, *Commercial Activities in the Indian Ocean*, 87.
79. *SII*, 8, 405 and 442; inscription of Valikandapuram (Tiruchi) dated 1207, reproduced in Karashima, *Commercial Activities in the Indian Ocean*, 268.
80. Shanmugam, 'Pattanapagudi' in Karashima, *Commercial Activities in the Indian Ocean*, 89–100.
81. Karashima and Kanazawa, 'Chinese Ceramic Sherds' in Karashima, *Commercial Activities in the Indian Ocean*, 109–114.
82. *SII*, 26, 635.

# GLOSSARY

*Ainnurruvar*: members of the merchant guild, Five Hundred

*Alvar*: Vaishnavite saint of the bhakti movement

*angadi*: market

*Anjuvannam*: a guild of foreign (Muslim) merchants

*brahmadeya*: Brahmin village

*chetti*: merchant, a generic term in the medieval period

*devadana*: donated to temples

*devakarmi*: temple officials

*disai-ayirattu-ainnurruvar*: merchant guild – Five Hundred of a Thousand directions

*eaglewood agil*: or aloes wood (Hobson-Jobson 335–36)

*erivirapattanam*: town of the armed warriors of the merchant guild

*grantha*: Tamil script with symbols for Sanskrit letters

*idaiyar*: shepherds

*Ilam*: Sri Lanka

*iraiyili*: tax free

*kadai*: shop

*Kadaram*: Tamil for Kedah, in Malay Peninsula

*kalanju*: gold, weight 80 grains; gold coin, equal to 2 kasu

*kalam*: large unit of volume; usually for measuring paddy

*kammalar* or *kanmalar*: artisan castes

*kasu*: gold coin

*kavarai*: merchant caste

*kottam*: administrative district under the Pallavas

*kudirai chetti*: horse trader

*magamai*: taxes

*Mahavamsa*: chronicle of Sri Lankan history

*malabathrum*: leaf of the cinnamon tree (Hobson-Jobson 543–44)

*malaimandalam*: hilly regions, Kerala

*managaram*: large city

*mandalam*: revenue sub-district under the Cholas

*manjadi*: gold coin, 1/8 kasu

*manradiar*: shepherds

*mayilatti*: a generic term for merchants

*meykirtti*: eulogy, at the beginning of inscriptions

*mlecchas*: barbarians

*muvendar*: the three kings of Tamilakam

*nadu*: sub-region above the village, and its assembly

*nagaram*: market town, and its assembly

*nagarattar*: members of the nagaram, merchants

*Nanadesi*: merchant guild, same as the Five Hundred

*nattar*: members of the nadu

*navaratna*: nine varieties of precious and semi-precious gems

*nigamam*: guild

*nigamattar*: members of a guild

*nilai poliyuttu*: permanent deposit

*nonda vilakku*:temple lamps which were lit continuously

*padinenbhumi*: merchant guild, lit. of the eighteen countries

*padinenvishayam*: merchant guild, lit. of the eighteen regions

*palisai*: interest

*pancasata virasasanam*: five hundred charters (of the guild)

*pattanapagudi*: assigned taxes, lit. share of the town

*perangadi*: the big market

*Perunkudi*: a class of merchants

*Perunteru*: main market street

*pon*: gold

*prasasti*: eulogy, at the beginning of inscriptions

*punniyam*: religious merit

*puravu vari*: department of revenue

*rakshai*: under the protection

*sabha*: assembly of the brahmadeya village

*sabhaiyar*: members of the sabha

*Sali*: saliyar weaving caste

*Sangam*: Classical school of Tamil literature

*Sankarappadi*: oil merchants

Savakam: Tamil for Java

*sonaka*: foreign (Arab) merchant

*spikenard (nard)*: fragrant ointment or oil (Hobson-Jobson 617–18)

*srikaryam arayginra*: official who supervised temple management

*sungam*: tolls, customs duties

*Tamilakam*: Tamil region

*Umanar*: salt merchants; salt makers

*Ur*: village (non-Brahman) and also the village assembly

*Urar*: members of the ur

*uri*: volumetric measure, usually for liquids like ghee

*valanadu*: revenue district under the Cholas

*Valanjiyar, vira Valanjiyar*: a merchant guild, from Sri Lanka

*vanikan*: merchant

*Vaniyar*: oil merchants

*variyam*: administrative committee

*velaikkara*: mercenary soldiers of the Chola army

*veli*: land measure, roughly 2.67 hectares

*velir*: minor chieftains

*Vellala*: landowning caste

*vihara*:Buddhist monastery

*virakkodiyar*: armed warriors employed by merchants

*vyapari*: merchant

*yavana*: Greeks or Romans

# BIBLIOGRAPHY

## Primary Sources

*Avanam. Tamil Tolliyal Kalagam*, Tanjavur.

*Manimekalai* by Sattanar. Ed. U.V. Swaminatha Iyer. Madras: U.V. Swaminatha Iyer Library, 1981. (7th edition.)

*Pattuppattu* (The Ten Songs). Ed. U.V. Swaminatha Iyer. Madras: U.V. Swaminatha Iyer Library, 1974.

*Maduraikkanchi*, by Mankudi Marutanar

*Malaipadukadam*, by Perumkausikanar

*Mullaippattu*, by Napputanar

*Nedunalvadai*, by Nakkirar

*Pattinappalai*, by Kadiyalur Uruththirankanninar

*Perumpanarruppadai*, by Kadiyalur Uruththirankanninar

*Porunarruppadai*, by Mudattamakkanniyar

*Sirupanarruppadai*, by Nallur Nattattanar

*Periplus of the Erythrean Sea*. Trans. and ed. Wilfred H. Schoff, 1912. (Reprint.) New Delhi: Oriental Reprint, 1974.

*Silappadikaram*, by Ilango Adigal. Ed. U.V. Swaminatha Iyer. Madras: U.V. Swaminatha Iyer Library, 1950.

*South Indian Inscriptions.* Archaeological Survey of India. Vols. 1–26.

Tirumangai Alvar. *Periya Tirumoli, Nalayira Divya Prabandam* (Four Thousand Sacred Verses).


## Secondary Sources

Abraham, Meera. *Two Medieval Merchant Guilds of South India.* New Delhi: Manohar, 1988.

Appadorai, A. *Economic Conditions in Southern India, 1000–1500 A.D.* 2 vols. Madras: University of Madras, 1936.

Champakalakshmi, R. 'Urbanisation in Medieval Tamil Nadu', in *Situating Indian History.* Ed. Sabyasachi Bhattacharya and Romila Thapar. Delhi: Oxford University Press, 1987. 34–105. (Also reprinted in *Trade, Ideology, Urbanization.*)

———. *Trade, Ideology, Urbanization: South India,* 300 B.C. to A.D. 1200. Delhi: Oxford University Press, 1996.

Curtin, Philip D. *Cross-Cultural Trade in World History.* Cambridge: Cambridge University Press, 1984.

Elliot, Walter. *Coins of Southern India.* (Reprint.) Delhi: Cosmo Publications, 1975.

Hall, Kenneth R. *Trade and Statecraft in the Age of the Colas.* New Delhi: Abhinav Publications, 1980.

*Hobson-Jobson: A Glossary of Colloquial Anglo-Indian Words and Phrases.* Ed. Henry Yule and A.C. Burnell. 1903. (Reprint.) Delhi: Munshiram Manoharlal, 1968.

Kanakasabhai, V. *The Tamils 1800 Years Ago*. 1904. (Reprint.)
New Delhi: Asian Educational Services, 1989.

Karashima, Noboru. *History and Society in South India: The
Cholas to Vijayanagar*. New Delhi: Oxford University
Press, 2001.

——. 'Tamil Inscriptions in Southeast Asia and China' in
*Commercial Activities in the Indian Ocean*. Ed. N.
Karashima. 10–18.

——. 'South Indian and Sri Lankan Inscriptions Relating to
the Merchant Guilds' in *Commercial Activities in the
Indian Ocean*. Ed. N. Karashima. 3–9.

——. Ed. *Ancient and Medieval Commercial Activities in the Indian
Ocean: Testimony of Inscriptions and Ceramic-sherds*. Tokyo:
Taisho University, 2002. (Report of the Taisho
University Research Project 1997–2000).

Karashima, N., and Y. Kanazawa, 'Testimony of Chinese
Ceramic Sherds' in *Commercial Activities in the Indian
Ocean*. Ed. N. Karashima. 109–14.

Karashima, N., and Y. Subbarayulu. 'A Trade Guild
Inscription from Viharehinna in Sri Lanka' and
'Ainnurruvar: A Supra-local Organization of South
Indian and Sri Lankan Merchants', *Commercial Activities
in the Indian Ocean*. Ed. N. Karashima. 27–39; 72–88.

Leur, J.C. van. *Indonesian Trade and Society*. The Hague: W.
van Hoeve, 1953.

Mahadevan, I. *Early Tamil Epigraphy from the Earliest Times to
the Sixth Century A.D.* Chennai: Cre-A and Harvard
University, 2003.

Maloney, Clarence. 'Archaeology in South India', in *Essays on South India*. Ed. Burton Stein. University of Hawaii, 1975. 1–40.

Majumdar, R.C. Ed. *History and Culture of the Indian People*. Bombay: Bharatiya Vidya Bhavan. Vol. 3, 1988; Vol. 4, 1993; Vol. 5, 1989. (First published 1954, 1955, 1957).

Minakshi, C. *Administration and Social Life under the Pallavas*. 1938. Madras: University of Madras, 1977. (Revised edition.)

Mukund, Kanakalatha. *The Trading World of the Tamil Merchant*. Hyderabad: Orient Longman, 1999.

Nilakanta Sastri, K.A. *Foreign Notices of South India from Megasthenes to Mahuan*. (Reprint.) Madras: University of Madras, 2001.

——. *A History of South India*. 4th ed. Madras: Oxford University Press, 1975.

——. *The Colas*. (Reprint.) Madras: University of Madras, 1984.

Pathmanathan, S. 'The Lankatilaka Temple Inscriptions of a Merchant Community', 'Nanadesis in Anuradhapura: A Unique Bronze Image of Virabhadra' and 'Trade and Urbanisation in Medieval Sri Lanka: The Virakoti Inscription at Budumuttava' in *Commercial Activities in the Indian Ocean*. Ed. N. Karashima. 36–47; 48–56; 62–71.

Raghava Aiyengar, M. 'The Ancient Dravidian Industries and Commerce' in *Tamilian Antiquary*. Ed. D.

Savariroyan. Vol. 1, part 8. 1910. (Reprint.) Delhi: Asian Educational Service, 1986. 75–100. (Tamil)

Ramesh, K.V. 'Reconsidering Cultural Intercourse between India and Southeast Asia: An Epigraphical Report' and 'Texts and Translations of Indian Inscriptions in Southeast Asia' in *Commercial Activities in the Indian Ocean*. Ed. N. Karashima. 147–59; 209–26.

Shanmugam, P. *The Revenue System of the Cholas. 850-1279*. Madras: New Era Publications, 1987.

——. 'Pattanapagudi: A Voluntary Impost of the Trade Guilds' in *Commercial Activities in the Indian Ocean*. Ed. N. Karashima. 89–100.

Spencer, George W. 'Temple Money-lending and Livestock Distribution in Early Tanjore'. *Indian Economic and Social History Review* 5(3): 277–93.

Stein, Burton. 'The Economic Function of a Medieval South Indian Temple' (reprinted in) *All the King's Mana: Papers on Medieval South Indian History*. Madras: New Era Publications, 1984. 68–82.

Subbarayalu, Y. 'The Tamil Merchant Guild Inscription at Barus, Indonesia: A Rediscovery' in *Commercial Activities in the Indian Ocean*. Ed. N. Karashima. 19–26.

Suresh, S. *Symbols of Trade: Roman and Pseudo-Roman Objects Found in India*. New Delhi: Manohar, 2004.

Tirumalai, R. *Land Grants and Agrarian Reactions in Cola and Pandya Times*. Madras: University of Madras: 1987.

# Introduction by Gurcharan Das

## *Arthashastra: The Science of Wealth*

### Thomas R. Trautmann

What is the secret of creating and sustaining wealth?

Ascribed to Kautilya (commonly identified as the prime minister of Chandragupta Maurya) and dating back more than 2000 years, the *Arthashastra* is the world's first manual in political economy. This book is intended to be an introduction to the economic philosophy of the *Arthashastra*, and its relevancy in the present times is indisputable.

## *Three Merchants of Bombay: Doing Business in Times of Change*

### Lakshmi Subramanian

How did the traders of Bombay shape capitalism in India?

*Three Merchants of Bombay* is the story of three intrepid merchants—Trawadi Arjunji Nathji, Jamsetjee Jeejeebhoy and Premchand Roychand—who traded out of Bombay in the nineteenth century, founding pioneering business empires, a proud milestone in the history of indigenous capitalism in India. This book traces that history and locates it in the greater narrative of the history of economic development in South Asia.

## Introduction by Gurcharan Das

### *The East India Company: The World's Most Powerful Corporation*

Tirthankar Roy

How did the East India Company change the way in which business was conducted in India?

For over 200 years, the East India Company was the largest and most powerful mercantile firm in Britain and Asia. Originally set up to procure Asian goods for British consumers, how and why did a merchant firm end up being an empire builder? This book answers these questions by taking a fresh look at the world of Indian business.

### *The Mouse Merchant: Money in Ancient India*

Arshia Sattar

What did ancient Indians think of money?

Even in ancient India, money is always a good thing and everyone wants it. The stories in *The Mouse Merchant*—selected from the Sanskrit universe, from the period of the late *Rig Veda* to the twelfth century—tell us how money was dealt with in everyday life in ancient and medieval Indian society. At the heart of these tales is the merchant. This book gives rare insights into the romance of the ancient seafaring life apart from imparting great wisdom about money.

## Introduction by Gurcharan Das

### *The Marwaris: From Jagat Seth to the Birlas*

Thomas A. Timberg

What is the secret behind the Marwaris' phenomenal business success?

In the nineteenth century, a tiny community from the deserts of Rajasthan spread out to every corner of India. Starting with inland trade and industry, Marwari businessmen account for a quarter of the Indian names on the *Forbes* billionaires list. What makes the Marwaris so successful? This book unravels the mystery.

### *Caravans: Indian Merchants on the Silk Road*

Scott C. Levi

The great adventure of the Multani merchants on the Silk Road to Central Asia

*Caravans* tells the fascinating story of the thousands of intrepid Multani and Shikarpuri merchants who risked everything to travel great distances and spend years of their lives pursuing their fortunes in foreign lands. The book examines the sophisticated techniques these merchants used to convert a modest amount of merchandise into vast portfolios of trade and also argues that the rising tide of European trade in the Indian Ocean usurped the overland 'Silk Road' trade and pushed Central Asia into economic isolation.